# Use It! Don't Lose It!

# MATH
## Daily Skills Practice
### Grade 6

by Jill Norris

**Incentive**Publications

*Illustrated by Kathleen Bullock*
*Cover by Geoffrey Brittingham*
*Edited by Cary Grayson*
*Copy edited by Steve Carlon*

ISBN 978-0-86530-665-3

3   4   5   6   7   8   9   10          09      08

PRINTED IN THE UNITED STATES OF AMERICA
www.incentivepublications.com

# Don't let those math skills get lost or rusty!

As a teacher you work hard to teach math skills to your students. Your students work hard to master them. Do you worry that your students will forget the material as you move on to the next concept?

If so, here's a plan for you and your students—one that will keep those skills sharp.

**Use It! Don't Lose It!** provides daily math practice for all the basic skills. There are five math problems a day, every day for 36 weeks. The skills are correlated to national and state standards.

Students practice all the sixth grade skills, concepts, and processes in a spiraling sequence. The plan starts with the simplest level of sixth grade skills, progressing gradually to higher-level tasks, as it continually circles around and back to the the same skills at a little higher level, again and again. Each time a skill shows up, it has a new context—requiring students to dig into their memories, recall what they know, and apply it to another situation.

## The Weekly Plan — Five Problems a Day for 36 Weeks

**Monday – Thursday** .............. • one computation item

| Monday – whole numbers | Wednesday – integers |
| Tuesday – decimals | Thursday – fractions |

• one problem-solving task (word problem)
• one algebra item

**Monday** and **Wednesday** ....... • one statistics or probability item
• one geometry item

**Tuesday** and **Thursday** .......... • one measurement item
• one number concepts item

**Friday** .................................... • two computation items
• one algebra item
• one item rotating among math strands
• one *Challenge Problem* demanding more involved steps, thinking skills, and calculations (making use of several skills)

## Contents

# How to Use Daily Skills Practice

To get started, reproduce each page, slice the Monday–Thursday lesson pages in half or prepare a transparency. The lessons can be used . . .

- **for independent practice**—Reproduce the lessons and let students work individually or in pairs to practice skills at the beginning or end of a math class.
- **for small group work**—Students can discuss and solve the problems together and agree on answers.
- **for the whole class review**—Make a transparency and work through the problems together as a class.

## Helpful Hints for Getting Started

- Though students may work alone on the items, always find a way to review and discuss the answers together. In each review, ask students to describe how they solved the problem-solving problems or other problems that involve choices of strategies.

- Allow more time for the Friday lesson. The Challenge Problem may take a little longer. Students can work in small groups to discover good strategies and correct answers for this problem.

- Provide measurement tools and other supplies students need for solving the problems. There will not be room on the sheet for all problems to be solved. Students will need scratch paper for their work.

- Decide ahead of time about the use of calculators. Since the emphasis is on students practicing their skills, it is recommended that the items be done without calculators and other calculation aids. If you want to focus specifically on technology skills, set a particular goal for certain lessons to be done or checked with calculators. You might allow calculator use for the Friday Challenge Problems.

- The daily lessons are designed to be completed in a short time period, so that they can be used along with your regular daily instruction. However, don't end the discussion until you are sure all students "get it," or at least until you know which ones don't get something and will need extra instruction. This will strengthen all the other work students do in math class.

- Keep a consistent focus on the strategies and processes for problem solving. Encourage students to explore and share different approaches for solving the problems. Explaining (orally or in writing) their problem-solving process is an important math skill. Be open to answers (correct ones, of course) that are not supplied in the Answer Key.

- Take note of which items leave some or all of the students confused or uncertain. This will alert you to which skills need more instruction.

- The daily lessons may include some topics or skills your students have not yet learned. In these cases, students may skip items. Or, you might encourage them to consider how the problem could be solved. Or, you might use the occasion for a short lesson that would get them started on this skill.

1. The base of the tent is a rectangle. The front measures 4' across, and the sides are twice as big. What is the perimeter of the base?

2. Solve the problem.

   **21,320 ÷ 65 =**

3. Choose the shape.
   - ○ pentagon
   - ○ hexagon
   - ○ trapezoid
   - ○ parallelogram

4. Choose the correct symbol.
   96 + −100 _____ 36 ÷ 9
   - ○ <   ○ >   ○ =

*I can really pack it in.*

5. Marie and Frank have to pack the lunch for *57* campers. They have the following supplies:
   - 171 sandwiches
   - 4 boxes of snack-size bags of chips (16 per box)
   - 5 dozen apples
   - 20 six-packs of bottled water
   - 8 cartons of candy bars (8 in a carton)

   Each lunch will be the same. They want to use as many of the supplies as they can. What should they put in each lunch? (Be sure to include quantities.) What leftovers will there be?

1. How many were involved in scouting?

   | **Annual Report** |
   | --- |
   | **988,995 scouts** |
   | **543,487 volunteer leaders** |

2. What is the value of the second eight in the number of scouts?

3. About how many scouts are enrolled in the program per volunteer leader?

4. Just before the evening campfire, the temperature was 65° F. When the scouts got up the next morning, the outdoor temperature had dropped 13 degrees. What was the temperature?

5. The scouts turned in their pledges for the walkathon. What was the total amount earned for the troop? What was the average amount earned?

   $ 16.82
   $ 67.52
   $ 85.01
   $ 93.72
   $  4.97
   $  9.50

*I'm a walk-a-thong.*

**1.** Ceci's troop made 800 first-aid kits for the flood victims. The kits must be packed in boxes that hold 12 kits. How many boxes can the troop fill? If the troop wants to fill each box completely, how many more kits should they make?

**2.** Five hundred of the first-aid kits are red and the others are black. What is the probability that the first recipient's kit will be red?

*I'm useful in an emergency.*

**3.** Choose the value that completes the statement.

$$72 = 4 \times \underline{\hspace{1cm}}$$

○ 76      ○ 68      ○ 18      ○ 288

**4.** Solve the problem.

$$47 - (-12) = \underline{\hspace{1.5cm}}$$

**5.** Number in order from least to greatest.

____ a. 53,172

____ b. 51,723

____ c. 57,132

____ d. 51,372

____ e. 52,371

*We're a bunch of happy campers.*

**1.** Fourteen leaders and 77 scouts will be forming teams for activities. Each team will have the same number of leaders and the same number of scouts. What is the greatest number of teams that can be formed? How many leaders will be in each group? How many scouts?

**2.** In all, 260 campers arrived at Camp La Foret on June 4. Three-quarters of the campers traveled by bus. How many campers did not ride the bus?

**3.** What information in problem two is not important to solving the problem?

**4.** Measure the length of the camp flag in centimeters.

**5.** Draw a factor tree to show the factors of 60.

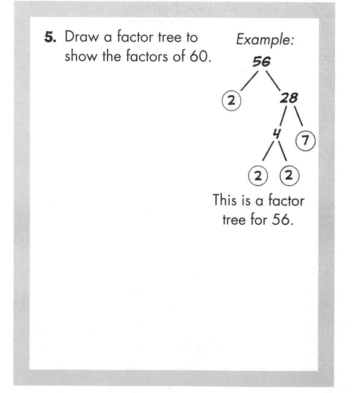

*Example:*

This is a factor tree for 56.

**6**

1. Choose the problem that is solved correctly.

   ○ –16 + 4 = –20      ○ 19 – (–10) = 29      ○ –30 = –10 + (–10) + 20      ○ –45 = –16 + 29

2. The scouts planted eight rows of sunflowers at the senior center. Each row had 27 plants. Write an equation to show the number of plants the scouts planted. Find the total.

I'm in row #7.
Where are you?

3. What is the next number in the pattern?

   **1    20    400    8,000** _____

4. Estimate the answer. Then find the difference. **50.2 – 0.99 = _____**

5. The table shows the number of tickets Felicia sold for the pancake breakfast. Make a graph showing the information.

   a. During which week did Felicia sell the most tickets?

   b. If her ticket sales follow the current trend, will they increase or decrease?

   c. If each ticket buyer eats two pancakes, how many pancakes are needed?

| Week | 1 | 2 | 3 | 4 | 5 |
|------|---|---|---|---|---|
| Tickets Sold | 22 | 35 | 33 | 46 | 44 |

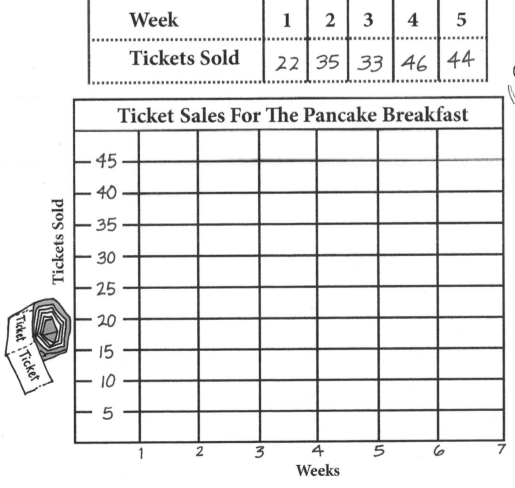

Ticket Sales For The Pancake Breakfast

*Name*

*Figure it out.*

**1.** Choose the correct property.

**a + b = b + a**
- ○ identity property
- ○ commutative property
- ○ associative property

**2.** There are 192 steps from the ground to the top of the pedestal where the Statue of Liberty stands, and 354 steps from the pedestal to her crown. How many steps must be climbed to enjoy the view from the crown? If the steps from the pedestal to the crown are divided into 22 stories, are there an equal number of steps between each story?

**3.** The guided tour of the statue takes about 45 minutes. When will the 11:50 a.m. tour be over?

**4.** You pay for snacks on the ferry with a $10.00 bill. The refreshments cost $5.76. Use an equation to find how much change you should receive.

**5.** For Grandma Carlon's 65th birthday, the family is going to Liberty Island to tour the Statue of Liberty. Mom and Dad, Baby Brett, ten-year-old Mattie, and seven-year-old Josh will go with Grandma. How much will they spend on ferry tickets?

**Ferry Ticket Prices**
Adult: $11.50
Senior: $9.50
(62 and older)
Child (4-12) $4.50
Under 4: Free

*Don't worry. You will see Lady Liberty when the fog lifts.*

*Name*

**1.** The Statue of Liberty is one heavy lady! Calculate the weight of each building material in tons.

- a. copper – 62,000 pounds
- b. steel – 250,000 pounds
- c. concrete – 54,000,000 pounds

**2.** Find the value of each expression.

**a. 3 x 1.2 + 4 x 2.6 = _____**

**b. 3.2 x 4.5 + 4.8 = _____**

**3.** Is **1,956** divisible by 3?
- ○ yes          ○ no

**4.** Write the words as a number in standard form.

**six million, four thousand thirty**

**5.** In a number square, the sum of the numbers in each row, column, and the two diagonals is the same.

- a. Find the sum for this square.
- b. Use the sum to write and solve equations to find the values of a, b, and c.

| 2 | 7 | c |
|---|---|---|
| a | 5 | 1 |
| 4 | b | 8 |

8

1. Write the rule for the function table.

| n | ? |
|---|---|
| 3 | 5 |
| 3.5 | 5.5 |
| 9 | 11 |

2. Each point of the star is an equilateral triangle. Determine the perimeter of:

   a. one triangle

   b. the pentagon in the center

6"

3. Solve the problem.

   **18 + ( −13) = _____**

Will it rain? . . . Or, won't It?

4. The weather forecaster is predicting that the probability of rain is 10 percent. Explain what that means.

5. The sixth graders at Frankie's school are going to visit the Statue of Liberty. There are seven classes of 32 students. The park rangers require one adult for every ten students. Students must stay with their chaperones at all times.

   a. How many adult chaperones will the sixth grade need?

   b. If the 90-minute tour has a limit of 38 participants, and 6 rangers are available to give tours simultaneously, how long will it take for all the sixth graders to finish the tour?

1. The Statue of Liberty officially celebrated her 100th birthday on October 28, 1986. How many years old is she today?

2. Write the expression in words as you would read it aloud.

   $$\frac{t}{4} + 1$$

A lady never tells her age.

3. Explain why seventy-two hundredths are equivalent to seven hundred twenty thousandths.

4. Lady Liberty's nose is 4' 6" long. How many inches is that? What classroom object is about the same length?

5. The photographer on the ferry charges the same price to take any group's photo. The photographer collected a total of $137.77 for the photographs shown in the line plot. Write and solve an equation to find the charge per photo.

```
                    X
    X               X
    X   X       X   X
    X   X   X   X   X
    X   X   X   X   X
    X   X   X   X   X
   ─────────────────────
    M   T   W   Th   F
```

**1.** Mark each equation true or false.

_____ **a. 48 ÷ 6 = 8**

_____ **b. 0.7 + 0.8 = 15**

_____ **c. 1.8 = 5.4 ÷ 3**

**2.** The ferry arrived at the dock at 8:42 a.m. Ana and Trevor had been waiting for eight minutes. Trevor had waited for Ana for six minutes before she arrived. What time did Trevor get to the dock?

**3.** Simplify the fraction. $\frac{18}{51}$ = _____

The Ferry arrived just in time.

**4.** Write **<** or **>** in each box.

**a.** −26 ☐ −14

**b.** −22 ☐ 22

**c.** −56 ☐ −65

## 5. Challenge Problem

Six friends sat at a table for the ferry ride to Liberty Island.

• Javier sat between Lindsey and Sue.

• Franco sat in seat 1. He is next to Pavi.

• Ellie is not beside Sue or Pavi.

Solve the problem to tell where the friends are sitting. Give two possible solutions.

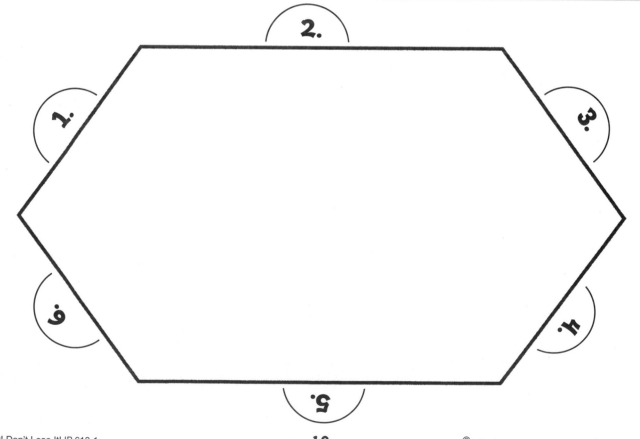

**1.** Round the number to the nearest hundred.

   **23, 749** _____

**2.** Which description matches this expression?

   **2 (14 + n)**

   ○ the product of a number and 14

   ○ the sum of 14 and a number

   ○ twice the sum of 14 and a number

   ○ a number divided by 14

**3.** What does this mean?

   **Scientists say that the probability of Nevado del Ruiz erupting is 100 percent.**

**4.** List three attributes of a square.

   a. _____

   b. _____

   c. _____

**5.** The top of the volcano is 425 feet above sea level. The base of the volcano is 654 feet below sea level.

   a. What is the height of the volcano? Draw a diagram that supports your answer.

   b. What can you infer about the location of the volcano?

Oops! I had jalapeños for lunch.

**1.** Express the decimal as a percent.

   **.75**

**2.** Choose the correct property.

   **a + (b + c) = (a + b) + c**

   ○ commutative property of addition

   ○ associative property of multiplication

   ○ associative property of addition

**3.** Mount St. Helens erupted in 1980 and in 2005. How many years were there between the eruptions?

**4.** Mount Fuji's last eruption was in 1708. How many years between Mount St. Helens' last eruption and Mount Fuji's last eruption?

I almost blew my stack,

...but I counted to 10.

**5.** Professor Vulcan started doing things from his to-do list at 6:00 a.m. If he takes a 25-minute break after inspecting the volcano vents, when will he finish his work?

**TO-DO LIST:**

CHECK SEISMIC READINGS......50 MIN.

INSPECT VOLCANO VENT........40 MIN.

ANSWER PHONE CALLS...........10 MIN.

**1.** Solve the equation. **x + 2 = 7**

**2.** Choose the number that is not a multiple of 5.

○ 40      ○ 75      ○ 64      ○ 15

**3.** What are the factors of 81?

*After a busy day erupting, ...I'm drained.*

**4.** Match the shapes to the correct labels.

____ rectangle    ____ parallelogram

____ octagon      ____ hexagon

a.        b.        c.        d.

**5.** Choose the best strategy for solving the problem.

**Three scientists take temperature readings each day. The chart represents the amount of time their observations take.**

| Scientist A | 1 hour, 35 minutes |
|---|---|
| Scientist B | 1 hour, 10 minutes |
| Scientist C | 55 minutes |

What is the average length of a reading?

○ Add the hours together. Add the minutes together. Divide by 3.

○ Change the hours to minutes and add the times together. Divide by 3.

○ Add the reading times together and subtract 3.

**1.** Write in simplest form. $4\frac{3}{8} - 1\frac{5}{16} =$ _____

**2.** Calculate the difference between a hot oven and the lava formed in a continent volcano.

**The temperature of lava depends on its composition. If it is the sort of lava that forms in undersea volcanoes, it is about 1200 degrees Celsius. If it is the sort of lava that forms on continent volcanoes it is cooler, only around 800 degrees Celsius. Your oven at home can go up to only about 250 degrees Celsius!**

**3.** Choose the problem that will result in the greatest quotient.

○ 0.082 ÷ 4        ○ 0.82 ÷ 8

○ 0.824 ÷ 12       ○ 8.2 ÷ 10

**4.** Circle the facts you need to solve the problem.

**While on vacation, Paul visited an inactive volcano. He collected samples of pumice. Pumice is a light, porous volcanic rock that forms during explosive eruptions. If Paul collects 24 pieces a day for two weeks, how many pieces will he have in his collection?**

**5.** Fill in missing values on the table.

Explain how the number of zeros in the standard form of a power of 10 relates to the exponent.

## Power Standard Form

| Power | Standard Form |
|---|---|
| $10^1$ | 10 |
| $10^2$ | 100 |
| $10^3$ | 1,000 |
| $10^4$ | a. |
| $10^{b.\_\_}$ | c. |
| $10^{d.\_\_}$ | e. |

### How Big are Volcanic Eruptions?

Scientists measure volcanoes using a Volcanic Explosivity Index (VEI). The index is based on a number of things that can be observed during an eruption.

**Read the VEI chart and answer the questions.**

| VEI | Description | Plume Height | Volume | How Often | Example |
|---|---|---|---|---|---|
| 0 | nonexplosive | < 100m | 100s m3 | daily | Kilauea |
| 1 | gentle | 100–1000m | 10,000s m3 | daily | Stromboli |
| 2 | explosive | 1–5 km | 1,000,000s m3 | weekly | Galeras, 1992 |
| 3 | severe | 3–15 km | 10,000,000s m3 | yearly | Ruiz, 1985 |
| 4 | cataclysmic | 10–25 km | 100,000,000s m3 | tens of years | Galunggung, 1982 |
| 5 | paroxysmal | > 25 km | 1km3 | hundreds of years | Mt. S. Helens, 1981 |
| 6 | colossal | > 25 km | 10 – 100 km3 | hundreds of years | Krakatau, 1883 |
| 7 | super-colossal | > 25 km | > 100 km3 | thousands of years | Tambora, 1815 |
| 8 | mega-colossal | > 25 km | > 1000 km3 | ten-thousands of years | Yellowstone |

1. What VEI rating did Mt. St. Helens' 1981 eruption receive?

2. What assumption does the chart support about how often really huge eruptions occur?

3. Howard thought that the numbers representing the volume of VEI 5, 6, 7, and 8 were smaller than VEI 0, 1, 2, 3, and 4 eruptions. Is he correct? Explain your response.

4. What is the difference between the volume of a **paroxysmal eruption** and a **cataclysmic eruption**?

## 5. Challenge Problem

Use the formula for finding the area of cone to estimate the area of the cinder cone volcano.

Area of a cone = $\frac{1}{3}$Bh where B = area of the base

Area of a circle = A = pi (3.14) x $r^2$

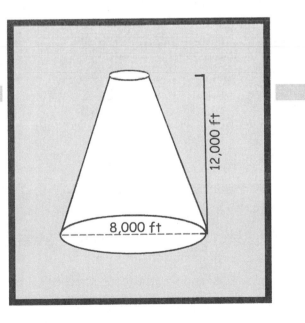

12,000 ft

8,000 ft

**1.** Name the property represented by the equation.

**7 + 0 = 7**

**2.** Find the value of **w** if **h = 4**.

**48 = 2(h + w)**

**3.** Round the number to the nearest ten thousand.

**168,932** _____

**4.** Solve the equation.

**2n = 36** _____

**5.** The puppet master has these four puppets. What is the probability of his using one of the two Durososonos?

○ $\frac{1}{4}$      ○ $\frac{1}{8}$

○ $\frac{1}{2}$      ○ $\frac{1}{3}$

**1.** Name the relationship between the two puppet shapes.

○ The figures are similar.

○ The figures are congruent.

**2.** Choose the correct answer. **33.7 x 4 = ?**

○ 13.48    ○ 134.8    ○ 13.38

**3.** Which unit would be the best choice for measuring the area of a puppet stage.

○ pounds    ○ square feet    ○ square inches

**4.** Ashawn will cut the wooden puppet rods. He needs eight rods. Four of the rods will be two feet long, two will be 18 inches, and two will be one foot long. How many feet of doweling should Ashawn buy?

**5.** A basic set of Wayang Kulit puppets includes over 100 puppets. Important characters will have several different versions in the set. If 20 percent of a set represents the same characters in different versions or poses, how many different characters are in a set?

1. Write a short definition of **probability**.

2. The details of the Wayang Kulit puppet are punched with a wooden mallet and sets of metal punches. If the puppet maker can make 100 punches in ten minutes and the puppet requires 8,000 punches, can he complete the punching in one hour? (Use mental math first, then check your answer.)

3. Starting at the fourth step, the puppet moved down three steps and then up eight steps. What step is the puppet on now?

4. Write three numbers that are between −4 and −6. Are all of these numbers **integers**? Explain.

5. Choose the two figures that are similar.

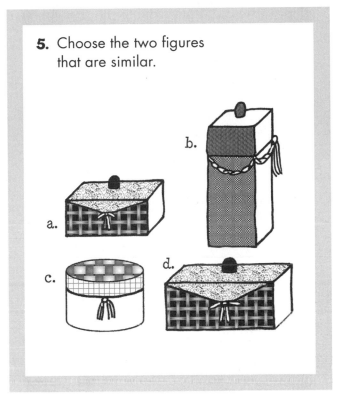

1. Choose the correct comparison.

   ○ $\frac{9}{2} > \frac{5}{6}$    ○ $\frac{9}{2} = \frac{5}{6}$    ○ $\frac{9}{2} < \frac{5}{6}$

2. Which equation is an example of the commutative property of multiplication?

   ○ $c \times b = b \times c$
   ○ $c(b + c) = cb + cc$
   ○ $c + 0 = c$
   ○ $c + b = b + c$

How many "times" have you used me?

3. Solve the equation.

   $$2(n + 2) - 8 = -28$$

4. Solve the problem.

   $$\frac{1}{2} + \frac{3}{8} = \_\_\_\_$$

5. Which measurement is most reasonable?
   a. weight of puppeteer    900 pounds
   b. weight of a vase        2 tons
   c. weight of a nut         3 ounces

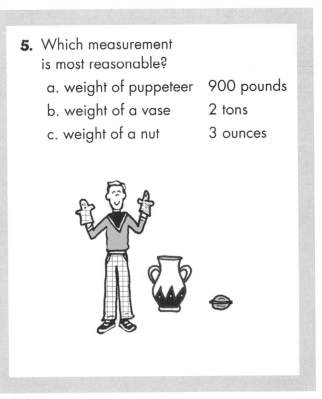

**1.** Choose the correct formula for finding the area and calculate it.

- ○ 12' x 16' = a
- ○ $\frac{1}{2}$(12') x 16' = a
- ○ 12' + 12" = 16' + 16' = a
- ○ 2(12') x 2(16') = a

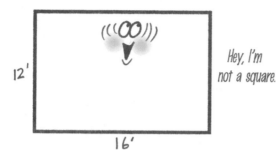

12'

16'

*Hey, I'm not a square.*

**2.** Which set of decimals is ordered from least to greatest?

- a. 0.2, 0.02, 0.22
- b. 0.24, 0.3, 0.05
- c. 0.15, 0.51, 1.05
- d. 0.49, 0.4, 0.05

**3.** Between which two numbers is the quotient **18.7 ÷ 5**?

- a. 2 and 3
- b. 3 and 4
- c. 4 and 5
- d. 5 and 6

**4.** Solve the problem.

**0.2 x 0.7 = _____**

## 5. Challenge Problem

One American dollar is equivalent to about 9,300 Indonesian rupiah. Determine the equivalent price of each item in American dollars. You can write a proportion to compare the currencies.

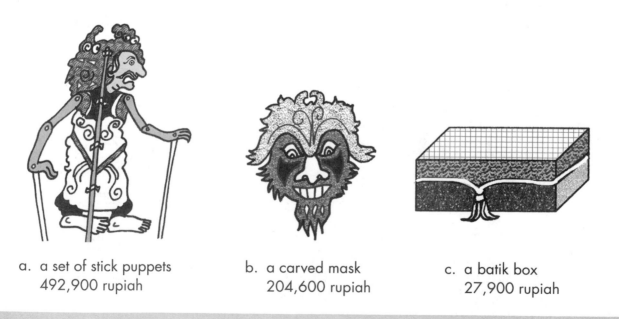

a. a set of stick puppets
492,900 rupiah

b. a carved mask
204,600 rupiah

c. a batik box
27,900 rupiah

**1.** One of the largest icebergs originated in Antarctica. It was about 208 miles long and about 60 miles wide. What was its area?

**2.** What is the value of the **7** in the number **3,506,487,210?**

**3.** a. What does the ratio $\frac{1}{5}$ mean?

b. Use the proportion $\frac{1}{5} = \frac{6}{x}$ to determine how many penguins there are on six icebergs.

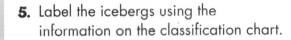

I feel like a birthday cake with five candles.

**4.** Tell whether each number is **prime** or **composite**.

a. 119

b. 231

**5.** a. About how many years are represented by the table of a glacier's life cycle?

b. What conclusion can you draw after looking at the table?

| Time | Iceberg Development |
|------|---------------------|
| **1000 BC** | Snow becomes firn |
| **950 BC** | Firn becomes glacier |
| | Glacier moves slowly seaward |
| **1990 AD** | Glacier calves—Large chunks break off to become icebergs |
| | Icebergs begin melting as ice falls into ocean |
| **1996 AD** | Iceberg melted |

**1.** List two common multiples of 8 and 12.

**2.** In 1985 the wreck of the Titanic was found at a depth of 12,612 feet. How many miles is that? (Round your answer to the nearest hundredth.)
*1 mile = 1,760 yards*

**3.** Choose the value that completes the inequality correctly.

$$3.15 + \underline{\quad} < 5$$

○ 1.95    ○ 1.85

○ 1.84    ○ 2.85

**4.** Solve the problem.

**34,567 – 488 = _____**

**5.** Label the icebergs using the information on the classification chart.

| Category | Height | Length |
|----------|--------|--------|
| Growler | less than 1m | less than 5m |
| Bergy Bit | 1–4m | 5–14m |
| Small | 5–15m | 15  60m |
| Medium | 16–45m | 61–122m |
| Large | 46–75m | 123–213m |
| Very Large | over 75m | over 213m |

a. Glacier 1    53m wide    _____

b. Glacier 2    4m long    _____

c. Glacier 3    13m wide    _____

d. Glacier 4    226m long    _____

I'm a Growler verging on a Bergy Bit.

Use It! Don't Lose It! IP 613-1

**1.** The Titanic sideswiped a great iceberg which gashed its hull. The flooded bow dipped into the water. A stack toppled, and three huge propellers lifted out of the water. The ship was tilted at about 45 degrees.

Choose the angle that represents the way the Titanic looked at this point.

a          b          c          d

**2.** Bridgit has four pairs of mittens: two pair are red, one pair is blue, and one pair is black. If she reaches into her mitten drawer and randomly chooses a mitten, what is the probability the mitten will be red?

*Do we match?*

**3.**        −9 x −8 = _____

**4.** Write the fraction in its simplest form.  $\frac{15}{35}$

**5.** Read the description of a tabular iceberg.

**Tabular Iceberg**
Steep sides with a flat top;
very solid;
length to height ratio
less than 5:1.

Draw a diagram to show an iceberg that would be classified as tabular. Give its height and length. Make sure the height and length fit the ratio of a tabular iceberg.

---

**1.** What would be the best tool for measuring the diameter of a snowball?

○ ruler       ○ meter stick       ○ tape measure

**2.** What day of the week is 260 days from Monday?

○ Monday          ○ Wednesday

○ Friday          ○ Tuesday

**3.** Find the quotient.  $\frac{9}{16} \div \frac{3}{4}$

**4.** The scientist left Antarctica on January 11 at noon to return home to the U.S. The trip takes 17 hours. What day will it be in Antarctica when she gets home to America?

*She won't get far on me.*

**5.** Mark each statement true or false. Justify your answer with statistics from the table.

____ a. Scientists failed to classify the size of almost half of the icebergs in the 1994 Ice Season.

____ b. The majority of the icebergs classified were large or very large.

____ c. Small and medium icebergs make up more than half of the number of those classified.

**Size Distribution of Icebergs**

| Size Category | % of total |
|---|---|
| Growler | 5.6% |
| Small | 15.3% |
| Medium | 15.3% |
| Large | 12.5% |
| Very Large | 2.8% |
| Size Unknown | 48.5% |

18

At 11:35 p.m. on April 14, 1912, the Titanic sank to the bottom of the Atlantic ocean. Thousands of passengers and crew died in the freezing cold waters of the Atlantic. The ship sideswiped a great iceberg and gashed its hull. The flooded bow dipped in the water. The smokestack toppled, and three huge propellers lifted out of the water. The ship was tilted at about 45 degrees. The steel fractured and the keel bent. The bows ripped loose, causing the stern to rise almost vertically and then slide downwards. The Titanic had 2,229 passengers and crew on board.

|  | 1st Class On Board | 1st Class Survived | 2nd Class On Board | 2nd Class Survived | 3rd Class On Board | 3rd Class Survived | Crew On Board | Crew Survived |
|---|---|---|---|---|---|---|---|---|
| Men | 175 | 57 | 168 | 14 | 462 | 75 |  | 192 |
| Women | 144 | 140 | 93 | 80 | 165 | 76 |  | 23 |
| Children | 6 | 5 | 24 | 24 | 79 | 27 |  |  |
| Total | 325 | 202 | 285 | 118 | 706 | 178 | 913 | 215 |

Use the chart to answer the following questions.

1. How many of the passengers were in third-class accommodations?

2. How many children in third class were lost?

3. How many crew members survived?

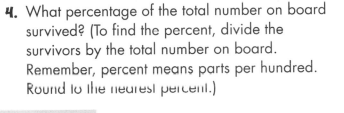

4. What percentage of the total number on board survived? (To find the percent, divide the survivors by the total number on board. Remember, percent means parts per hundred. Round to the nearest percent.)

## 5. Challenge Problem

Complete the graph to show the information on the table.

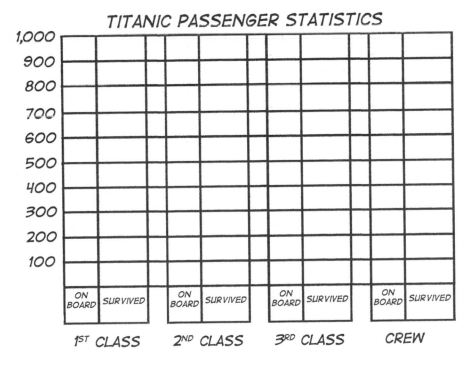

TITANIC PASSENGER STATISTICS

**1.** Round the number to the nearest hundred thousand.

**6,845,209**

**2.** Solve the equation.

**x + 16 = 35**

**3.** In all, $16,800 was collected from chocolate sales at the carnival. If each chocolate bar cost $1.75, how many chocolate bars were sold?

○ 7,900 chocolate bars

○ 8,900 chocolate bars

○ 9,600 chocolate bars

○ 960 chocolate bars

**4.** Find the surface area of a pan of brownies 9" square.

**5.** a. Which two figures are **congruent**?

   b. Which two figures are **similar**?

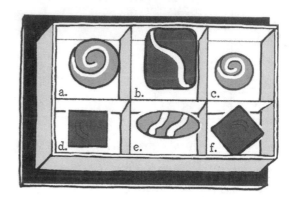

**1.** Express the decimal as a percent.

**1.35**

**2.** Which object would weigh about five pounds?

   ○ a bag of chocolate chips

   ○ a Valentine box of chocolates

   ○ a life-size chocolate replica of a taxi cab

**3.** The regular price of the chocolate taxi was $2,500. It is on sale for 50 percent off. How much will the taxi cost now?

**4. 26.3 x 28 = _____**

Nothing says "I love you" like a chocolate kiss.

I love you, too.

**5.** Choose the best strategy for solving the problem.

**Trina's backpack holds a bottle of chocolate milk (12 oz), a chocolate-colored sweatshirt (1 lb), two candy bars (8 oz each), and an "I love chocolate!" cap (9 oz.). What is the total weight of the pack's contents?**

a. Change all the weights to ounces. Add them together. Express the answer in pounds and ounces.

b. Change all the weights to grams. Then add them together. Express the answer in kilograms.

c. Just add the weights together. (It won't matter if the numbers represent ounces or pounds.)

1. Estimate the size of this angle.

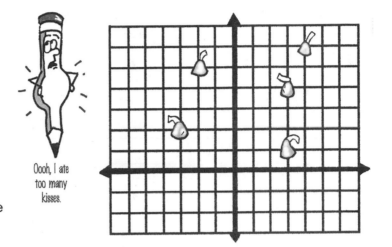

B

2. Choose the best label.
   ○ a pair of parallel lines
   ○ perpendicular lines
   ○ intersecting lines

3. The bowl of chocolate candies has 12 red candies, 12 white candies, and 24 pink candies.

   a. How many possible outcomes exist when you randomly select a candy?

   b. What are the chances of choosing a red candy? a pink candy?

   c. Do the chances change after $\frac{1}{2}$ of the candies have been eaten?

4. Solve the equation. **2r + 5 = –21**

**5.** Write the correct coordinates for each chocolate kiss.

Oooh, I ate too many kisses.

---

1. Solve the problem.

   $\frac{2}{3} + \frac{4}{5} =$ _____

2. Choose the number that is not a multiple of 3.
   ○ 30      ○ 14      ○ 24   ○ 42

3. Which group is correct?

   a. $\frac{9}{2} < 3\frac{1}{3} < \frac{4}{9}$

   b. $\frac{4}{9} < \frac{9}{2} < 3\frac{1}{3}$

   c. $\frac{4}{9} < 3\frac{1}{3} < \frac{9}{2}$

4. Write each expression using an exponent.
   a. 5 x 5 x 5
   b. 2 x 2 x 2 x 2 x 2
   c. 1.5 x 1.5

I'll bet you didn't calculate on that.

**5.** The campers decided to make s'mores, but they had a little trouble with the marshmallows. They dropped a total of 35 into the campfire. Bo dropped three of them. Dan dropped four times as many as Bo and Charlie together. How many did Charlie drop?

It's marshmallow madness!

## Nothing says "Thanks" like a brownie à la mode!

**1.** Miss T wants to serve Muffin Cup Brownies for the parents' reception. Mr. Burnham estimates there will be 150 parents attending. Miss T's recipe serves 12. How many batches of brownies will Miss T have to make?

*Miss T*

*Mr. Hamberg*

**2.** If Miss T serves brownies, Mr. Hamberg will bring the ice cream. He estimates that he can get 50 scoops from each gallon. How many gallons will he need if he plans to give everyone one scoop?

*Mr. Steve*

**3.** Mr. Steve will bring milk and coffee. In all, 74 percent of the parents prefer coffee. How many servings of coffee should he plan on preparing?

**4.** Mr. Burnham will handle the plates, napkins, and spoons. He can buy them by the gross. How many of each should he purchase?

*Mr. Burnham*

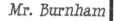

### Recipe:

### Ingredients

$\frac{2}{3}$ cup sifted flour

$\frac{1}{2}$ teaspoon baking powder

$\frac{1}{4}$ teaspoon salt

$\frac{1}{3}$ cup butter

2 ounces cocoa powder

2 tablespoons hot water

1 cup sugar

2 eggs, beaten

$\frac{1}{2}$ cup coarsely chopped pecans

1 teaspoon vanilla

Preheat oven to 350 degrees. Grease 12 muffin cups. Sift flour with baking powder and salt. Sift again. Melt butter in water. Stir in cocoa powder.

In a mixing bowl, beat eggs. Beat in sugar until well-blended. Blend in chocolate mixture. Stir in flour mixture until well-mixed. Stir in vanilla and pecans. Fill muffin cups about $\frac{1}{3}$ full. Bake for 20 to 25 minutes. Cool. Makes 12 round muffin brownies.

**5.** Miss T is going shopping to buy her ingredients. Please complete her shopping list.

### Grocery List:
___bags of flour (5 lb bag)
___bags of sugar (5 lb bag)
___boxes of butter (4 cubes to a box)
___bottles of vanilla (4 oz. bottle)
___tins of cocoa powder (12 oz. tin)
___cartons of eggs (dozen)

**Hints:** *My grandma says, "A pint's a pound."*
*Two cubes of butter make one cup (16 tablespoons).*
*One cup equals 8 oz.   One gross is 12 dozen.*
*Three teaspoons equal one tablespoon. Two tablespoons equal one ounce.*

**1.** Round the number to the nearest hundred.

**7,643,950**

**2.** Solve the equation.

**7y = 5(21)**

*I'm a Millenium Falcon Model.*

**3.** Steve purchased a Millenium Falcon and a Pod. The cost of the Falcon was ten times the cost of the Pod. Steve paid $110.00. Set up an equation to show how to find the cost of the Pod. What is the cost of the Pod?

**4.** Choose the correct formula for finding the area. Then solve the problem.

- ○  10" x 5" = a
- ○  $\frac{1}{2}$(10" + 5") = a
- ○  $\frac{1}{2}$(10") x 5" = a
- ○  2(10") + 5" = a

**5.** Match the statistical term with its definition.

_____ a. the average of the data

_____ b. the difference between the least and the greatest numbers

_____ c. the number that appears most often

_____ d. the number in the middle of the data set

_____ **median**    _____ **mean**

_____ **mode**    _____ **range**

**1.** Express the percentage as a decimal.

**6%**

**2.** Choose the set of numbers that represent factors of 102.

a. 7, 2, 3

b. 34, 6, 17

c. 51, 8, 102

**3.** Solve the problem.

$78.80
+ 36.20
=

**4.** Solve the problem.

**26.3 x 28 = _____**

**5.** Look at the graph. Answer the questions.

Each whole tile = 100 LEGOs.

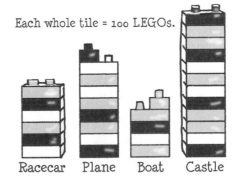

Racecar   Plane   Boat   Castle

a. What is the range of LEGOS used in the projects?

b. What is the mean of the data?

**1.** Estimate the size of this angle.

    a. 30 degrees

    b. 90 degrees

    c. 155 degrees

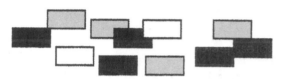

**2.** Which statement is the most reasonable?

    a. The box for my small set of Legos was four yards long.

    b. My pencil is one yard long.

    c. The playground is 100 yards long.

**3.** Solve the problem.

$$-6 \times -12 = \underline{\hspace{1cm}}$$

**4.** If you build a column of about 40,000,000,000 LEGO bricks, it would reach the moon. Write the number as a power of ten.

**5.** Ahmed has 11 LEGO blocks in his hand: five are white, four are red, and two are red. What are the odds that the one he will use is red?

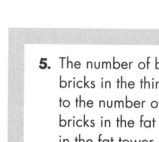

**1.** Solve the problem.

$$\frac{1}{2} + \frac{5}{6} =$$

**2.** Thomas bought two building sets for $64.00. One set cost $40.00, and the second set was on sale for 50 percent off. What was the original price of the second set?

**3.** If seven LEGO sets are sold each second, how many LEGO sets are sold in three hours?

**4.** Measure the log.

    (Give its length to the nearest half-inch.)

Let go of my LEGO.

**5.** The number of black bricks to white bricks in the thin tower is proportional to the number of black bricks to white bricks in the fat tower. Color the bricks in the fat tower accordingly.

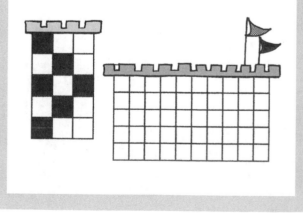

Choose the correct comparisons.

1. ○ $\frac{7}{9} < \frac{2}{3}$

   ○ $\frac{2}{3} = \frac{7}{9}$

   ○ $\frac{2}{3} < \frac{7}{9}$

2. ○ $\frac{4}{5} < \frac{7}{9}$

   ○ $\frac{4}{5} = \frac{7}{9}$

   ○ $\frac{7}{9} < \frac{4}{5}$

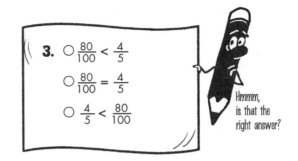

3. ○ $\frac{80}{100} < \frac{4}{5}$

   ○ $\frac{80}{100} = \frac{4}{5}$

   ○ $\frac{4}{5} < \frac{80}{100}$

Hmmm, is that the right answer?

4. Children spend five billion hours a year playing with LEGO bricks. How many days is that? (Round to the nearest day.)

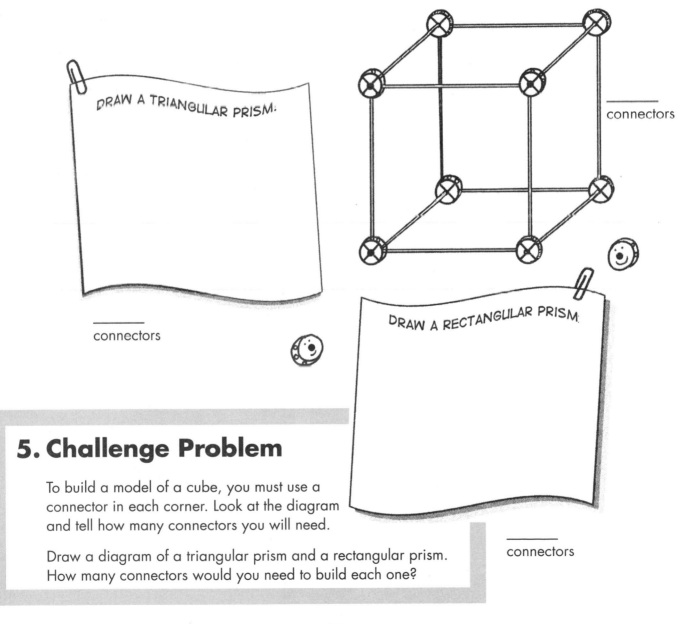

DRAW A TRIANGULAR PRISM:

_____ connectors

_____ connectors

DRAW A RECTANGULAR PRISM:

## 5. Challenge Problem

To build a model of a cube, you must use a connector in each corner. Look at the diagram and tell how many connectors you will need.

Draw a diagram of a triangular prism and a rectangular prism. How many connectors would you need to build each one?

_____ connectors

Use It! Don't Lose It! IP 613-1

1. Elise wants to buy an iPod for $200.00 and a deluxe carrying case for $75.00. She will use the $50,00 gift card she received for Christmas. How much will she owe?

2. Write the formula for finding the desktop area. Is the desktop more or less than two square feet?

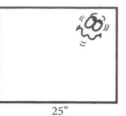

20"

25"

3. Write the fractions in simplest form.

   **a.** $\frac{15}{25}$        **b.** $\frac{16}{56}$        **c.** $\frac{36}{54}$

4. Estimate to decide. Between which two numbers is the quotient **18.7 ÷ 5**?

   ○ 2 and 3        ○ 3 and 4        ○ 4 and 5

5. Tom and Alex accessed the same Website for downloading their screensaver. If there were five different screensavers available, and each boy chose the one he wanted independently of the other, what is the probability that they chose the same screensaver?
[Hint: Use this formula:
P(event A) x P(event B) = answer.]

Let me choose.

1. Bev's computer applications took up 25 percent of the space on her 160 GB hard drive. How much space is being used by applications?

2. Choose the correct answer.

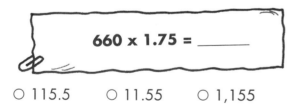

   **660 x 1.75 = _____**

   ○ 115.5        ○ 11.55        ○ 1,155

3. It is estimated that the number of PCs in use worldwide will top one billion in 2007. Write one billion in exponential form.

4. The top 15 countries in the world in terms of PC usage have a total of 822,150,000 PCs. Write the number using expanded notation.

5. Trisha's new laptop weighs four pounds. Her dad's older laptop weighs six pounds. How much less does Trisha's laptop weigh? How many ounces is that?

I'm very PC.

**1.** What is the chance of randomly choosing a month that begins with the letter **J**?

**2.** Which property is represented by the equation?

$$3 \times (5 \times 2) = (3 \times 5) \times 2$$

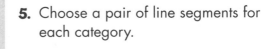

I once lived in Bill Gates' pocket protector.

**3.** Choose the number closest to $\frac{1}{2}$.

○ $\frac{3}{4}$

○ $\frac{3}{8}$

○ $\frac{3}{9}$

○ $\frac{3}{10}$

**4.** Bill Gates was born on October 28, 1955. He went to Harvard University in September, 1973. How old was he?

**5.** Choose a pair of line segments for each category.

_____ **parallel lines**

_____ **perpendicular**

_____ **intersecting**

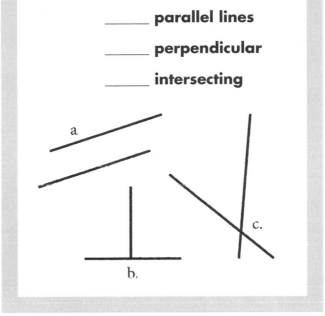

---

**1.** Solve the problem.

$$\frac{2}{3} - \frac{1}{4} = \underline{\quad\quad}$$

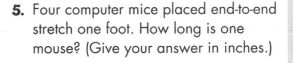

**2.** Which unit would be the best choice to measure the length of the computer cable?

○ pounds and inches

○ feet and yards

○ miles and cups

**3.** Choose the number that is not a multiple of 12.

○ 48    ○ 64

○ 72    ○ 108

**4.** Find the value of **b** if **h** is equal to four.

$$36 = \frac{1}{3} \, bh$$

**5.** Four computer mice placed end-to-end stretch one foot. How long is one mouse? (Give your answer in inches.)

These look nothing like the mice I know.

## Personal Computer Use - Top **10** Countries

| Year-end 2004 | PCs in use (in millions) | Share of worldwide number (rounded to nearest percent) |
|---|---|---|
| United States | 223.81 | 27% |
| Japan | 69.20 | 8% |
| China | 52.99 | 6% |
| Germany | 46.30 | 6% |
| United Kingdom | 35.89 | 4% |
| France | 29.41 | 4% |
| South Korea | 26.20 | 3% |
| Italy | 22.65 | 3% |
| Canada | 22.39 | 3% |
| Brazil | 19.35 | 2% |

*Facts from Computer Industry Almanac, March 2005*

There are clones of me around the world.

**1.** Write the number of personal computers (PCs) in use in the United States.

**2.** Write the number of PCs in use in Japan.

**3.** What is the difference between the two?

**4.** One out of three PCs in the United States is a laptop or notebook. How many laptops are in use in the United States? (Round your answer to the nearest thousand.)

## 5. Challenge Problem

Create a circle graph to show the relationship of Personal Computer Use between the top five countries. Follow these steps:

a. Round the top five countries' PC usage number to the nearest million.

b. Add the usage numbers to find how many computers the whole circle represents.

c. Divide the whole number into eighths.

d. Using the divided circle and the PC usage numbers, plot the five countries on the circle.

e. Label and color the graph.

PCs have put a lot of pencils out of business.

**1.** Solve the equation.

**2x = 88**

**2.** Choose a common multiple of 8 and 7.

○ 48          ○ 15          ○ 560

**3.** Robert made three trips up the ladder to the tree house. Tristan made six trips up the ladder. Mark and Kyle each made five trips. Chris made only two trips. What was the average number of trips made?

**4.** Joy is securing the netting to the side of the tree house. If the railing is six feet long, and she is putting a tie every four inches, how many white ties will she need to finish her pattern?

**5.** The platform of the tree house is an L-shape. What is the platform's perimeter? Area?

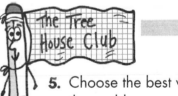

**1.** Express the decimal as a percent.

.04

**2.** Rhia pays $68.40 for the plans for a tree house. Her friend Fran paid only 85 percent of that amount. How much did Fran pay?

**3.** The roof protects the tree house. The guidebook recommends an 18" overhang. If the tree house platform is a 5' x 6' rectangle, what size rectangle will be formed by the bottom edge of the roof?

**4.** The guidebook also recommends a pitch of 45 degrees. Which diagram shows a roof that would fit this specification?

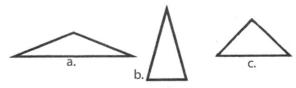

**5.** Choose the best way to solve the problem.

**Bob and Brett are making three flags for their tree house. They need 48 feet of wood doweling for the supports. The hobby store sells the special wooden dowels at $2.00 per four-foot dowel. How much will the boys have to spend on wood?**

a. Multiply 48 by $2.00.

b. Divide 48 by 4 and multiply by $2.00.

c. Multiply $2.00 by 4 and divide that number into 48.

**1.** Write the unit rate as a ratio. Then find an equal ratio.

    a. The cost is $6.75 for one item. Find the cost of eight items.

    b. There are three feet in one yard. Find the number of feet in 15 yards.

    c. There are 9 rungs on the ladder. Find the number of steps on seven ladders.

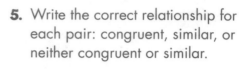
Climb the ladder of success.

**2.** –4.5 x 9.3 =

**3.** Choose the missing operation.

    96 ÷ 24 ____ 4 = 16

    ○ +       ○ x       ○ –

**4.** Write the next three terms in the number pattern.

    4  12  36  108  _____ _____ _____

**5.** Write the correct relationship for each pair: congruent, similar, or neither congruent or similar.

    a. Figure a and Figure b

    b. Figure c and Figure d

    c. Figure c and Figure e

    d. Figure a and Figure d

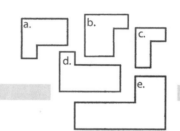

**1.** $\frac{3}{4} - \frac{1}{6} =$

**2.** Solve the equation. **x – 5.7 = 5.7**

**3.** Which of the following operations would you use to isolate the variable in **x + 6 = 27**?

    a. Add 6 to both sides.

    b. Subtract 6 from both sides.

    c. Add 27 to both sides.

    d. Subtract 27 from both sides.

**4.** Write and solve an equation to find the number of plans the tree house gang sold.

    **The tree house gang is selling plans to earn money for a new rope ladder. They get $.35 profit for each plan they sell. The club's total profit is $14.70.**

... and then he makes like a tree, and leaves.

Heh, heh.

**5.** Trina created a snack spinner for her tree house. She spins to see what snack to eat.

    a. If she spins once, which snack is most likely?

    b. Which snack is least likely?

    c. How many possible outcomes are there?

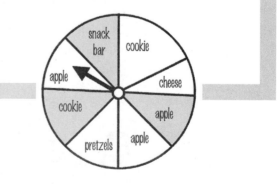

The boys drew a plan for their tree house on graph paper. They made it a scale drawing. Each square equals ten inches. Look at the plan they have drawn and answer the questions.

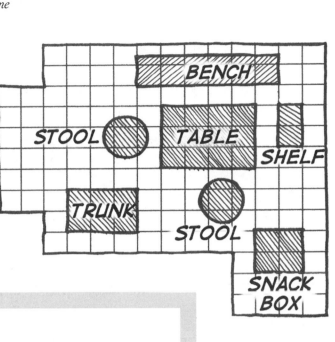

**1.** How far is the table from the snack box?

**2.** How big is the table? Express your answer in feet and inches.

**3.** Is it realistic to move a second bench the same size as the first one into the tree house?

**4.** What is the area of the tabletop?

## 5. Challenge Problem

Use the graph paper diagram. Arrange the six items in the tree house. Draw each item on the diagram. Make each one to scale.

- table (3' square)
- bookshelf (12" x 36")
- cot (5' x 3')
- two cubes for sitting (18" square)
- trunk for storage (4' x 2')

2 squares = 1 foot

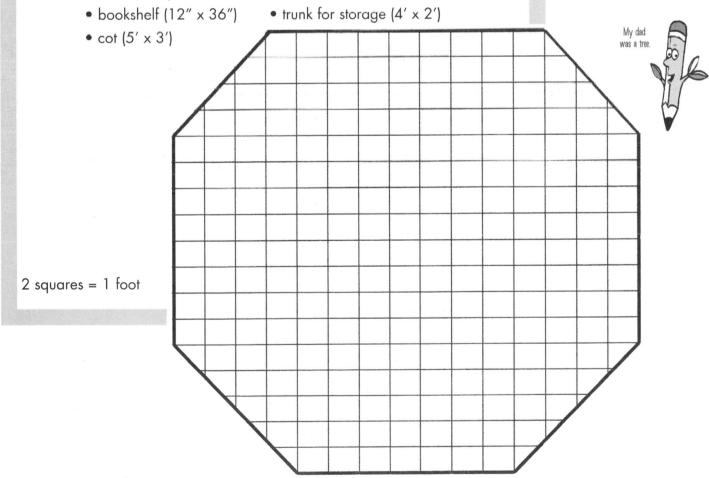

My dad was a tree.

1. Round to estimate the answer. Then solve the problem.

$$24{,}576 \div 48 =$$

*Sometimes I feel like a dim bulb.*

2. Recycling one can saves enough electricity to light a 100-watt bulb for 3.5 hours. How many cans would have to be recycled to light the bulb for a full day?

3. Write an algebraic expression for each word phrase.

    a. 10 more than k

    b. 30 times n

    c. 20 divided by r

4. Name the figure.

5. Use the table to answer the questions.

**Individual State Waste Management Performance**

| Rank | Best Management (tons/person/year) | | Worst Management (tons/person/year) | |
|---|---|---|---|---|
| 1. | South Dakota | 0.400 | Nevada | 2.132 |
| 2. | Wisconsin | 0.580 | Kansas | 1.879 |
| 3. | North Dakota | 0.628 | South Carolina | 1.588 |
| 4. | Colorado | 0.649 | Delaware | 1.491 |
| 5. | Oklahoma | 0.663 | Utah | 1.484 |
| 6. | Minnesota | 0.679 | New Hampshire | 1.471 |
| 7. | Idaho | 0.732 | Indiana | 1.432 |
| 8. | Missouri | 0.761 | Hawaii | 1.342 |
| 9. | Louisiana | 0.769 | Georgia | 1.333 |
| 10. | Maine | 0.784 | Missouri | 1.316 |

a. What does the number under *best* and *worst* represent?

b. What is the difference between the state with the best waste management and the worst waste management?

c. What is the difference between Maine and South Dakota's waste management? How many pounds of waste is that?

# TUESDAY WEEK 10 _____ MATH PRACTICE

*Name*

1. California generates about 45,000,000 tons of waste per year. How many pounds of waste is that? Write the number as a power of ten.

2. Tell whether each equation is true or false.

    a. $0.7 + 0.8 = 15$

    b. $1.8 = 5.4 \div 3$

    c. $6.5 \times 3.4 = 2.21$

3. Evaluate the expression for **x = 7**.

$$(x + 3) - 4$$

4. Tennessee recycles 40 percent of its waste. Tennessee generates 9,496,000 tons of waste per year. How much does the state recycle?

*Quick! Recycle me!*

5. Check the problems. Correct the ones that are solved incorrectly. Round to the nearest cent.

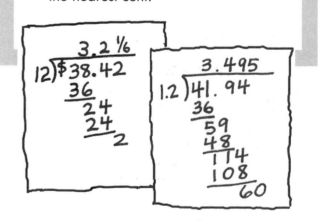

**1.** Solve the problem by drawing a diagram.

> Todd is stacking recycled shoeboxes. He stacks them in a pyramid shape. If the pattern continues, how many shoeboxes will be in a stack eight boxes high?

**2.** True or false?

> The product of two negative integers is a negative integer.

*I guess you can't have too many shoes.*

**3.** Write the mathematical expression in words.

**y – 8**

**4.** Recycling a ton of glass saves the equivalent of nine gallons of fuel oil. The Avery Farm fills their 100-gallon fuel oil tank twice during the winter months. Is it reasonable to say that the farm's glass recycling could pay for their fuel oil costs? Explain your answer.

**5.** Name the shape. Write a formula for determining its perimeter. Measure the length of one side in centimeters. Then use the measurement and the formula to find the perimeter.

**1.** How many minutes are in 3 hours and 25 minutes?

**2.** Write the next three numbers in the pattern. Explain your reasoning.

$1\frac{1}{2}$, $2\frac{1}{4}$, 3, $3\frac{3}{4}$, $4\frac{1}{2}$,

_____, _____, _____

**3.** Which number is closest to five?

a. $4\frac{3}{4}$          c. $4\frac{7}{8}$

b. $4\frac{2}{6}$          d. $4\frac{1}{3}$

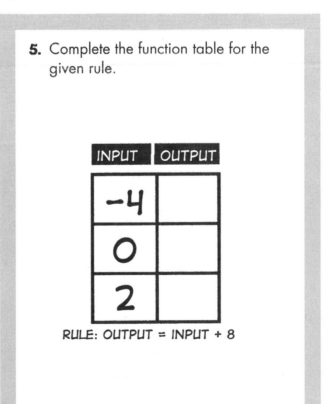

*I'm a recycle volunteer.*

**4.** The average household throws away 45 kg of plastic a year. Five percent of the plastic thrown away is recycled. How much plastic is recycled in an average household?

**5.** Complete the function table for the given rule.

| INPUT | OUTPUT |
|-------|--------|
| -4    |        |
| 0     |        |
| 2     |        |

RULE: OUTPUT = INPUT + 8

*Name*

1. Solve the problem.        $-19 + (-9) =$

2. What is the lowest common multiple of 12 and 15.

3. At the community garden, the planting committee has decided to plant a row of tomato plants along the back fence. The fence is 60 feet long. If they place the plants 30 inches apart, how many plants will they have room for?

Are tomatoes fruits or vegetables? Or, are they just delicious?

4. Solve the equation.

   $x + 2.4 = 2.7$

# 5. Challenge Problem

The recycling trucks pick up plastic from the collection bin every three days and glass every five days.

a. Suppose both items are picked up today. In how many days will both items again be picked up on the same day? Write an explanation of how you solved the problem.

b. Suppose both items are picked up on a Sunday. How many Mondays will pass before the pickup is on a Monday again?

Get into a recycling cycle.

**1.** How many leopard frog offspring survive in one year?

   **One Northern leopard frog produces 5,000–6,000 offspring annually. However, only about ten percent of the offspring survive.**

**2.** Write an expression for each word phrase.
   a. 8 plus k
   b. 10 decreased by n
   c. 43 less than h
   d. 17 times m

**3.** Estimate each product by rounding to the nearest whole number.
   a. 2.25 x 13.76
   b. 2.449 x 3.47

**4.** What is the value of **6x ÷ 2** when **x = 9**?

I'm a survivor.

**5.** Find the area of the parallelogram.

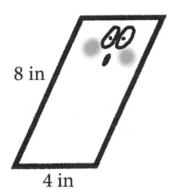

8 in

4 in

**1.** Solve for n.

   **n − 10.6 = 12.8**

**2.** The spotted turtle produces 3–4 offspring annually. If one turtle pair has three babies, and the babies each have three babies for eight years, how many will there be (assuming that all the turtles survive)?

You could say I come from a big family.

**3.** Is 17,595 divisible by 9?

**4.** Write a rule for determining where to put the decimal place when multiplying two decimals.

**5.** A biologist studying the ecology of a river makes a weekly shortnose sturgeon count. Find the mean number of fish counted in a week.

| Week: | Sturgeon |
|-------|----------|
| 1 | 19 |
| 2 | 18 |
| 3 | 22 |
| 4 | 23 |
| 5 | 20 |
| 6 | 24 |
| 7 | 23 |
| 8 | 20 |
| 9 | 34 |
| 10 | 19 |

**1.** Name the opposite of each integer.

   a. 13

   b. –8

   c. 150

**2.** Solve the problem.    **8 + (–11) = ____**

**3.** The African elephant is a threatened species, and the Asian elephant is an endangered species. An adult female elephant's height is about 5.5 times the length of her hind footprint. Use an equation to find the approximate height of an adult female elephant whose hind footprint is 1.5 feet long.

**4.** The ranger leads a nature walk every Saturday. If the probability of sighting a spring peeper on the walk is 60 percent, how many times should the ranger expect to see a spring peeper on 30 nature walks?

**5.** Draw a line of symmetry for each symmetrical figure. Tell whether the line you drew is the only line of symmetry possible for that figure.

**1.** Write three fractions equivalent to each fraction.

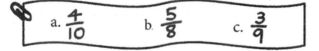

   a. $\frac{4}{10}$      b. $\frac{5}{8}$      c. $\frac{3}{9}$

**2.** Which of the following does NOT describe the expression **n – 45**?

   a. n minus 45          c. n less than 45

   b. 45 subtracted from n    d. 45 less than n

**3.** The giant tortoise traveled $7\frac{1}{3}$ yards and $8\frac{1}{2}$ yards. What is the total distance the tortoise traveled?

**4.** A giant tortoise's top speed is about $\frac{1}{5}$ mile per hour. Estimate how long will it take the tortoise to travel across its habitat. (one mile = 1,760 yards)

420 ft

**5.** Draw a tree diagram to find the two-digit permutations you can make with the digits 7, 8, and 9. Use each digit once in each permutation.

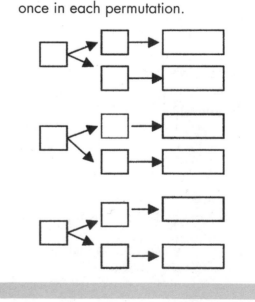

1. Write the first six terms in the pattern.
   Start with 3.2 and multiply by 5 repeatedly.

2. Solve the problem.

   **1.8 x 4.302 =**

3. Write each number in standard form.

   **a. two hundred sixteen**

   **b. two hundred twenty-two thousandths**

   **c. two hundred sixty-one**

   **d. two and sixteen hundredths**

4. Use mental math to solve each equation.

   **a. 30 = y + 1**

   **b. n – 6 = 16**

   **c. a ÷ 5 = 5**

   **d. 194 = 10a**

## 5. Challenge Problem

Arrange the digits 1 – 9 in the boxes on the triangle so the sum of the numbers along each side is 17.

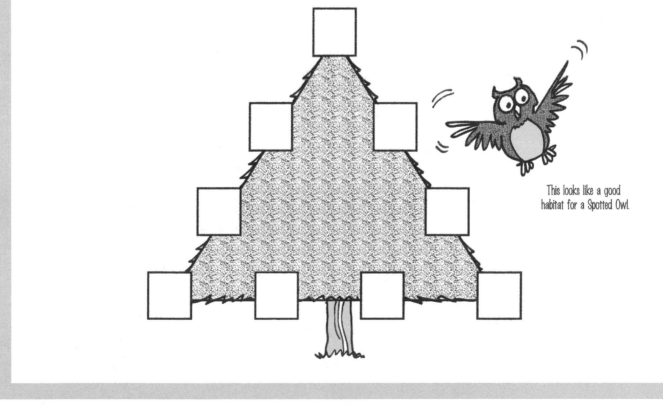

This looks like a good habitat for a Spotted Owl.

1. The Panama Canal has a work force of about 9,000 employees and operates 24 hours a day, 365 days a year. Write a formula for finding the number of man-hours the work force puts in each year. Then solve the equation.

2. Round the number to the nearest thousand

    **854,672**

3. Solve the problem.

    **98,742 − 79,875 = _____**

4. Solve the problem.

    **98,742 + 79,875 = _____**

*I know the answer!*

5. The Coral Princess paid the amount of $226,194.25 to pass through the canal. Write an equation to determine how much per kilometer the passage cost. The canal is 80 kilometers long.

    Richard Halliburton paid the lowest toll for crossing the canal. He paid 36 cents to swim across. How much did he pay per kilometer?

1. The Panama Canal is approximately 80 kilometers long. It was cut through one of the narrow saddles of the isthmus that joins North and South America. How long is the canal in miles?

2. Solve the problem.

    **5.68 + 3.008 = _____**

    *1 kilometer = .621 miles*

3. Solve the equation.

    $$\frac{y}{1.6} = 0.256$$

4. Choose the value of $(5 + 6)^2 − 1$.
    a. 16      c. 40
    b. 30      d. 120

5. Last year about 14,000 vessels used the Panama Canal. In fact, commercial transportation activities through the Canal represented approximately five percent of world trade. If the percentage of trade using the canal increased to ten percent, and the actual amount of trade stayed the same, how many vessels would use the canal?

**1.** Choose the statement that is not true.

○ −9 < −7    ○ −3 < 5

○ −5 > −3    ○ −2 < 6

**2.** The US Marine hydrofoil Pegasus made the fastest transit of the Panama Canal. It took the racing boat just 2 hours and 41 minutes. About what was Pegasus's average speed? Round the answer to the nearest kilometer per hour. Remember, the canal is 80 kilometers long.

**3.** Use an integer to represent each situation.

a. fares collected equaling $5,400.00

b. 25 feet below water level

c. a debt of $15.00

**4.** Solve the problem. **(−8) + 12 + (−5) = ___**

**5.** The Panama Canal uses a system of locks, compartments with entrance and exit gates. The locks work as water lifts. They raise ships from sea level (the Pacific Ocean or the Atlantic Ocean) to the level of Gatun Lake (26 meters above sea level). Draw a diagram to show how a ship moves. Express the change in elevation in negative and positive integers.

**1.** Solve the problem.

$$9\frac{2}{3} - 5\frac{2}{3} = \underline{\quad}$$

**2.** Solve the problem.

$$9\frac{1}{8} - 6\frac{3}{4} = \underline{\quad}$$

**3.** Explain how you can use mental math to find the answer.

$$6\frac{1}{4} - 3\frac{3}{4}.$$

**4.** More than 922,000 vessels used the Panama Canal between August 1914 and August 2005. What is the average number of vessels per year? (Round your answer to the nearest vessel.) Is it reasonable to assume that the same number of vessels went through the canal each year? Explain your answer.

**5.** The Panama Canal cost Americans around $375,000,000.00. It was the single most expensive construction project in United States history at the time of the canal's completion. Do you have enough information to find out the cost of the canal per American taxpayer? If not, what information do you need?

Bill: $375,000,000.00

The taxpayers are going to be shocked when they get this bill.

Use the information on the table. Decide whether the facts support the following statements. Mark the statements true or false.

1. _____ The last month of the construction required the greatest number of workers.

2. _____ The number of workers in December 1911 was almost double the number in December 1906.

3. _____ Wages were paid for 100,000 workers in June 1912, August 1913, and June 1914.

4. _____ During the initial stages of construction, fewer workers were employed than were employed in the final stages.

### Panama Canal Construction Workers

| Selected Months and Years | Work Force *(rounded to the nearest hundred)* | Selected Months and Years | Work Force *(rounded to the nearest hundred)* |
|---|---|---|---|
| May 1904 | 1,000 | October 1909 | 35,500 |
| November 1904 | 3,500 | March 1910 | 38,700 |
| November 1905 | 17,000 | December 1911 | 37,800 |
| December 1906 | 23,900 | June 1912 | 38,200 |
| October 1907 | 32,000 | August 1913 | 40,000 |
| April 1908 | 33,200 | June 1914 | 33,300 |

## 5. Challenge Problem

In 1906, some 6,500 of the workers were from Barbados. What percentage of December 1906's workforce came from Barbados? Round your answer to the nearest tenth.

Make a graph that tracks the number of construction workers. Don't forget to title your graph.

NUMBERS OF WORKERS ON THE PANAMA CANAL FROM 1904–1914

45,000
40,000
35,000
30,000
25,000
20.000
15.000
10,000
5,000

DATES

1. Wrigley Field in Chicago is the oldest National League ballpark and Fenway Park is the oldest American League ballpark. What is the difference in their ages? (Ignore Leap Years.)

   **First game at Wrigley – April 23, 1914**
   **First game at Fenway – April 20, 1912**

2. The ice cream vendor at the ballpark sells two sizes of cones. During one batting practice, he sold 46 regular cones at $2.00 each and 28 double-dip cones at $3.00 each. How much money did he collect?

3. The executive parking lot at the ballpark forms an L shape. What is the area of the lot?

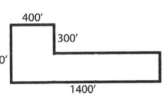

400'
300'
600'
1400'

4. Choose the set of numbers that represent factors of 18.

   ○ 3, 5, 7    ○ 1, 9, 3    ○ 6, 2, 0

5. Javier strikes out twice in a nine-inning game. How many times will he strike out in 48 innings if he strikes out the same number of times proportionally?

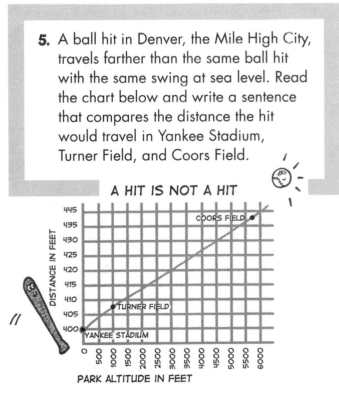

1. Which property is represented by this equation?

   **4 x (6 + 3) = (4 x 6) + (4 x 3)**

   _____

2. Find the difference.

   $ 89.00
   - 36.29

3. Choose the name of the shape of the ballfield.

   ○ hexagon
   ○ pentagon
   ○ octagon

4. Solve the problem.

   **206.08 divided by 64 = _____**

5. A ball hit in Denver, the Mile High City, travels farther than the same ball hit with the same swing at sea level. Read the chart below and write a sentence that compares the distance the hit would travel in Yankee Stadium, Turner Field, and Coors Field.

A HIT IS NOT A HIT

COORS FIELD
TURNER FIELD
YANKEE STADIUM

DISTANCE IN FEET
445 435 430 425 420 415 410 405 400

PARK ALTITUDE IN FEET
0 500 1000 1500 2000 2500 3000 3500 4000 4500 5000 5500 6000

Use It! Don't Lose It! IP 613-1

1. Solve the problem.

   **6 yd 1 ft 7 in + 1 ft 11 in =**

Pull a ticket
out of my hat.

2. The radius of the on-deck circle is 1.5 ft. What is the area of the circle?

3. Sierra will draw a ticket to see where she will sit to see the game. In the basket are five tickets for the first balcony, three tickets for the box seat level, six tickets for the rock pile, and six tickets for the second balcony. What are the odds that she will sit in the first balcony?

4. Find the value of **x** if **b = 25**

   **225 = 3(b + x)**

5. The coach spent a total of $7,956.00 on bat-boy uniforms. If each uniform cost $110.50, how many uniforms did the coach buy?

   Estimate the answer first and then solve the problem.

1. A third-base line box ticket to a playoff game at Bank One Ballpark costs $375.00, and the same ticket costs $600.00 at Busch Stadium. Which would cost more, four box tickets to a game in Bank One Ballpark, or three tickets in Busch Stadium?

2. Choose the correct comparison.

   a. $\frac{14}{36} > \frac{7}{18}$

   b. $\frac{14}{36} = \frac{7}{18}$

   c. $\frac{14}{36} < \frac{7}{18}$

3. Complete the equality.

   $7\frac{1}{2}$ **cups = _____ pints**

4. Write each fraction in its simplest form.

   a. $\frac{4}{14}$          b. $\frac{6}{18}$          c. $\frac{8}{10}$

5. There are $1\frac{1}{3}$ times as many girls as there are boys in the group. If there are 18 boys, how many people are in the group. Explain how you got your answer.

Use the chart with statistics about National League Ballparks to answer the questions.

| Ballpark Names | Team Name | First Game | Seats | LF | CF | RF |
|---|---|---|---|---|---|---|
| Bank One Ballpark | Arizona Diamondbacks | 3/31/1998 | 48,500 | 328' | 402' | 335' |
| Busch Stadium | St. Louis Cardinals | 5/16/1966 | 49,625 | 330' | 402' | 330' |
| Citizens Bank Park | Philadelphia Phillies | 4/12/2004 | 43,500 | 329' | 401' | 330' |
| Coors Field | Colorado Rockies | 4/26/1995 | 50,381 | 347' | 415' | 350' |
| Dolphins Stadium | Florida Marlins | 4/05/1993 | 42,531 | 335' | 410' | 345' |
| Great American Ballpark | Cincinnati Reds | 3/31/2003 | 42,059 | 328' | 404' | 325' |
| Dodger Stadium | Los Angeles Dodgers | 4/10/1962 | 56,000 | 330' | 395' | 330' |
| Miller Park | Milwaukee Brewers | 4/06/2001 | 43,000 | 342' | 400' | 345' |
| Minute Maid Park | Houston Astros | 4/07/2000 | 42,000 | 315' | 435' | 326' |
| PETCO Park | San Diego Padres | 4/08/2004 | 42,445 | 367' | 396' | 382' |
| PNC Park | Pittsburgh Pirates | 4/09/2001 | 38,127 | 325' | 399' | 320' |
| RFK Stadium | Washington Nationals | 4/09/1962 | 56,500 | 335' | 410' | 335' |
| SBC Park | San Francisco Giants | 4/11/2000 | 40,800 | 335' | 404' | 307' |
| Shea Stadium | New York Yankees | 4/17/1964 | 55,777 | 338' | 410' | 338' |
| Turner Field | Atlanta Braves | 4/12/1997 | 50,062 | 335' | 401' | 330' |
| Wrigley Field | Chicago Cubs | 4/23/1914 | 38,902 | 355' | 400' | 353' |

Choose five ballparks. Use the statistics to determine:

**1.** the average length from home plate to the centerfield fence

**2.** average number of seats

**3.** the park that has been used for the most years

**4.** the park where a hitter who hits straight away to center field would like to try for a homerun

# 5. Challenge Problem

Design your own ballpark. Provide the statistics for an entry in the chart above. Each number you choose must be within the range of the current parks.

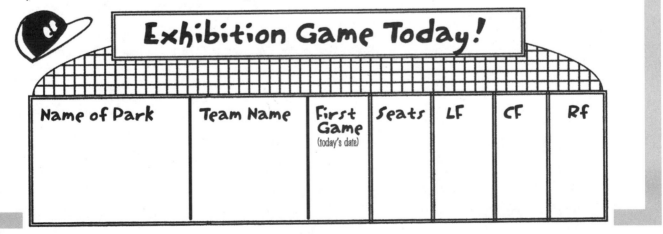

## Exhibition Game Today!

| Name of Park | Team Name | First Game (today's date) | Seats | LF | CF | Rf |
|---|---|---|---|---|---|---|
| | | | | | | |

**1.** Choose the ordered pair for **P**.

○ (3, 2)   ○ (–2, –3)

○ (2, –2)   ○ (–3, 2)

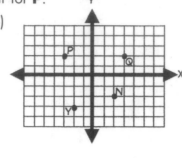

**2.** Correct the problem.

```
    8,472
  x    38
   67266
   28416
  351,426
```

**3.** What is the GFC of 40 and 72?

**4.** What is the median of the set of **4, 7, 9, 13, 25?**

My pony left without me.

**5.** Mark the facts you need to know to solve the problem. Then solve it.

**How long will it take a Pony Express rider to go from Elwood to Granada?**

a. The average speed of a galloping horse is 35 mph.

b. Riders are between 11 and 45 years old.

c. A horse can gallop for ten miles before slowing down.

d. The distance between Granada and Elwood is 61 miles.

e. 183 men ride for the Pony Express.

f. Riders change horses every ten miles.

g. It takes two minutes to change horses.

**1.** Estimate each amount.

**a. 20 % of 98**

**b. 6 % of $19.89**

**c. 15% of $34.56**

WANTED
Pony
Express
Riders

**2.** Solve for z.

**z + 6 = 8.2**

**3.** What is the value of **23 x 32?**

**4.** Find the product.

**7.0005 x 10 =**

**5.** Calculate the largest possible weight of a Pony Express rider.

mail pouch, mail = 20 lbs

saddle, blanket, halter = 20 lbs

rider  = ___ lbs

_____

Maximum Load = 165 pounds

I carry quite a load.

**1.** Find the difference.

   a. $-2 - (-12)$

   b. $16 - (-21)$

   c. $-4 - 17$

I'm his favorite shirt.

**2.** Suppose the pony express rider had more than one kind of shirt and more than one pair of jeans. Which of the following could not be the total number of outfits he could wear?

   a. 3   b. 6   c. 9   d. 12

**3.** Order the numbers from least to greatest.

   **7.  70  .770  770  .077  −77  −7.7**

**4.** What do the statistics tell you about how the value of a dollar has changed?

   **The cost of sending a letter by Pony Express was about $5.00. Based on today's dollars, the cost of a letter would have been about $75.00.**

**5.** Look at the patterns. There are several attributes that form each one. Draw the next figure in each pattern.

   a.  p P q Q r R s

   b.  ▯▯▯ ●●●● ●●●● ▯▯▯ ●●●● ●●●●

   c.  ❖❖ ⌘ ❖❖❖ ⌘ ❖❖❖❖

**1.** Use tree diagrams to find the two-digit permutations with the digits 2, 4, 6, and 8. How many permutations are possible?

**2.** Order the numbers from the least to the greatest.

   $\frac{17}{40}$     $\frac{7}{20}$     $\frac{5}{16}$

**3.** Find the difference.

$\frac{7}{10} - \frac{1}{4}$

I'm lying down on the job.

**4.** Find the sum.

   $2\frac{1}{6} + 5\frac{3}{8}$

**5.** Measure the horse's shoe. Then use the scale to determine the real size.

   **1 cm = $3\frac{1}{2}$"**

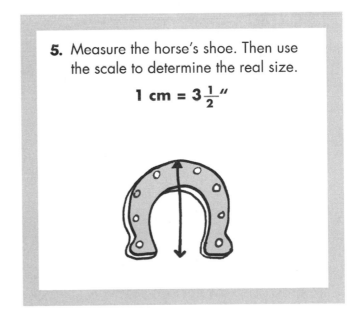

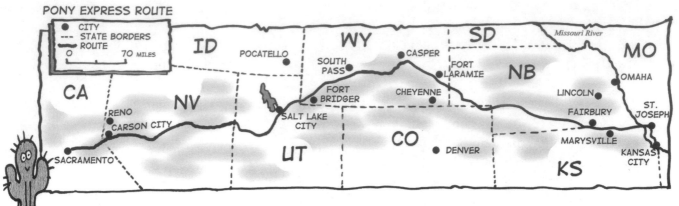

1. Pony Express stations were placed at intervals of about ten miles along the route. How many stations would be located on the route from Maryville to Salt Lake City.

2. If a rider changed horses at every station, how many horses would it take to complete the ride from Carson City to Sacramento

3. How many miles is the route from St. Joseph to Fairbury?

4. Is it reasonable to expect one rider to complete the whole route? Explain.

## 5. Challenge Problem

Design a new mail route. It must begin in Cheyenne. It must have no more than seven stations. Name your route. Tell how many horses will be needed for one trip. Tell how long the trip will take.

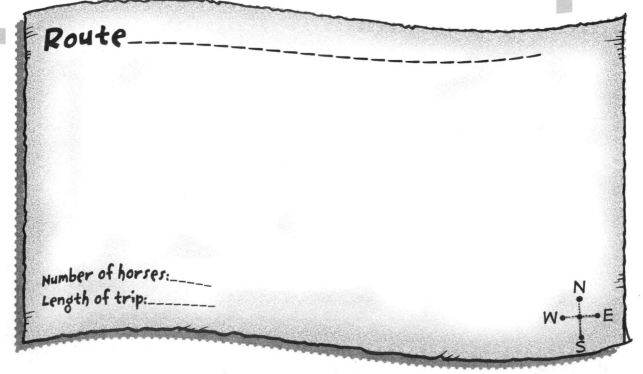

Route _ _ _ _ _ _ _ _ _ _ _ _ _ _ _ _ _

Number of horses: _ _ _ _ _ _
Length of trip: _ _ _ _ _ _ _ _

1. Test each number for divisibility by 3.

    a. 57

    b. 92

    c. 171

2. Name the parallel lines.

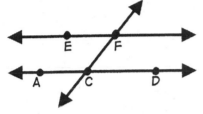

3. Solve the problem.

    **89,451 x 305 = _____**

4. Explain what the term **3 cubed** means.

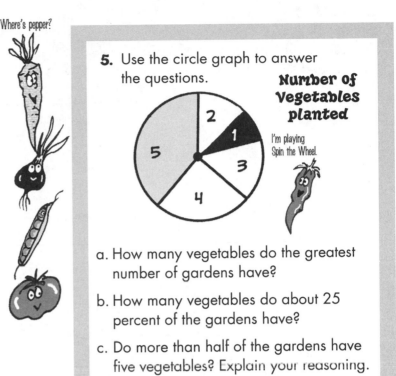

*Where's pepper?*

5. Use the circle graph to answer the questions.

    **Number of Vegetables planted**

    *I'm playing Spin the Wheel.*

    a. How many vegetables do the greatest number of gardens have?

    b. How many vegetables do about 25 percent of the gardens have?

    c. Do more than half of the gardens have five vegetables? Explain your reasoning.

1. Evaluate the expression for **a = 1.5**.

    **10a divided by 3**

2. Find the elapsed time between 7:15 a.m. and 1:45 p.m. Explain how you got your answer.

3. Choose the largest number.

    ○ 25% of 81

    ○ 40% of 63

    ○ 85% of 35

4. Find the median of the data set.

    **8, 35, 13, 7, 62, 81, 20**

5. Carlos and Marie are the Weekend Weeders. Carlos earns $44.55 for nine hours work. Marie earns $50.40 in 12 hours. What does Carlos get paid for an hour of work? What does Marie get paid per hour? If the two worked together and received the same rate, what would the charge per hour be for the two weeders?

*Weeds have feelings, too.*

WEED PULLERS NEEDED

1. Sandy is digging a posthole for her scarecrow. She has already dug ten inches, and the hole needs to be two feet deep. Think of ground level as 0 and express the amount she has dug as an integer. How many more inches does she need to dig?

2. What is the circumference of Mr. Huff's herb garden?

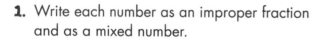

12 m

**C = πd**

3. Solve the problem. **(−4) x 5 =**

4. Peter has four pumpkin seeds, three radish seeds, and five cucumber seeds. He is randomly planting one seed at a time. What are the odds of his planting two pumpkin seeds in a row?

5. Draw the fourth figure in the pattern.

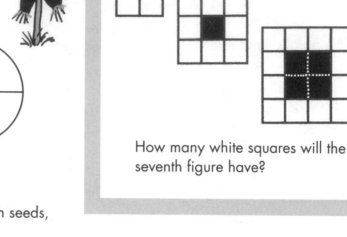

How many white squares will the seventh figure have?

1. Write each number as an improper fraction and as a mixed number.

   a. **seven-fifths**
   b. **nine-sixths**
   c. **fifteen-eighths**

What do you mean, improper?

2. Solve the problem. $\frac{3}{7}$ x $\frac{5}{9}$ =

3. Jose is planting a garden that is a rectangle $5\frac{1}{3}$ x $6\frac{3}{4}$ feet. What is the area? What is the perimeter?

4. Which sentence represents the **commutative property** of multiplication?

   a. (3 x 2) x 4 = 3 x (2 x 4)
   b. 4 x (7 + 2) = 4 x 9
   c. 6 x 4 = 4 x 6

5. Mr. Sutter used one half bottle of liquid fertilizer on his roses. If the bottle holds one pint of fertilizer, how many ounces did he use?

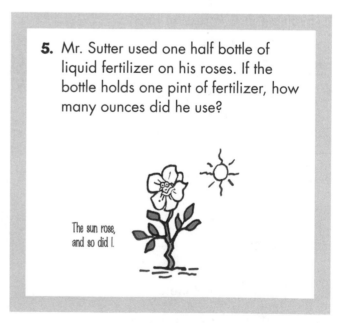

The sun rose, and so did I.

1. A gardener is building a border for a garden with a row of paving stones. The row is $37\frac{1}{2}$ feet long. Each paving stone is 15 inches long.

   a. How many paving stones does the gardener need?

   b. If each paving stone costs $.75, how much will the border cost?

2. The paving stones come in green, brown, and cream. The gardener wants to use two colors. How many different combinations of two colors can he choose? What are they?

3. Design a pattern for the border using two colors and sixteen bricks.

4. Add a second row to the border using the same two colors, but with a different pattern.

## 5. Challenge Problem

Design the shape of a garden. It must have a perimeter of 58 feet and at least three sides. What is the area of your garden? Does changing the shape of your garden change the area? Give examples to support your answer.

My Garden

Use It! Don't Lose It! IP 613-1

# MONDAY WEEK 16 _____ MATH PRACTICE

*Name*

**1.**

$$8,908$$
$$- 6,289$$

**2.** Which problem is correct?
   a. 670 x 4 = 8620
   b. 5 x 937 = 4,865
   c. 374 x 7 = 2,618

**3.** Solve the equation.

   $q \div 6 = 4$

**4.** Write all the possible names for this figure. Circle the most definitive name.

**5.** A 20-foot anaconda weighs 550 pounds. A 25-foot reticulated python weighs 10.5 pounds per foot. How much does the reticulated python weigh? If these two snakes are typical of their species, what statement can you make about their lengths and weights?

# TUESDAY WEEK 16 _____ MATH PRACTICE

*Name*

**1.** The body of an anaconda has a diameter of 12 inches. What is the circumference of the snake?

**2.** $2,048.8 \div 8 =$

**3.** The pet shop is selling a ball python for $43.00. If the tax is seven percent, what will the cost of the snake be?

**4.** Measure the snake's body in inches. Give your answer to the nearest $\frac{1}{4}$ inch.

**5.** The line plot shows the number of babies each mother python hatched.
   a. Find the median.
   b. In all, how many babies were hatched?
   c. What is the range of the number of babies hatched?

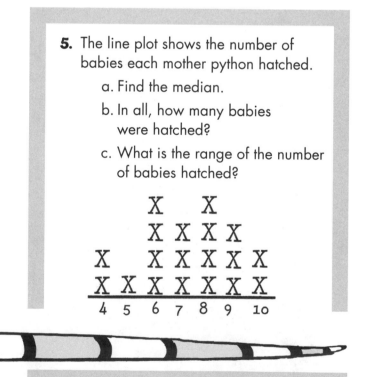

```
        X       X
        X   X   X   X
  X     X   X   X   X
  X X   X   X   X   X   X
  4  5  6  7  8  9  10
```

**50**

1. Solve the problem. **(–4) x 5 = ?**

2. Sam took a quiz on caring for snakes. In scoring the quiz, he added points for correct answers and deducted points for incorrect answers. If he missed the first three 20-point questions and then answered four 10-point questions correctly, what is his score? Write your answer as an integer.

3. The Caramel Blush is a new breed of albino python. One breeder reported a 1 in 16 chance for hatching a Caramel Blush. If he breeds four female pythons, and each mother has four offspring, how many Caramel Blush pythons will hatch?

4. Name the figure's shape.

5. Read the information and then answer the question.
**Caring for a big snake is a big job. The enclosure must be big enough for the snake and its water bowl, hiding place, basking area, etc. The snake's cage must be kept warm. Two thermometers (one in the cool area and one in the basking area) will assure that the snake is kept comfortable.**

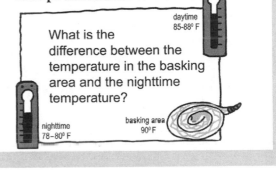

What is the difference between the temperature in the basking area and the nighttime temperature?

daytime 85-88° F

nighttime 78–80° F

basking area 90° F

1. Write each fraction in its simplest form.

   a. $\frac{15}{35}$

   b. $\frac{21}{49}$

   c. $\frac{18}{72}$

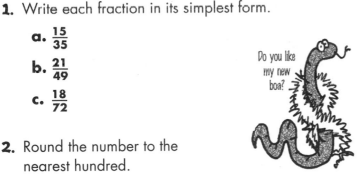

Do you like my new boa?

2. Round the number to the nearest hundred.

   **89,998** _____

3. Simplify the inequality.

   **b – 3 > 12**

4. Thirteen is subtracted from a number. The result is greater than 9. Write an inequality to describe the situation.

5. The record length for the reticulated python is 33 feet. How many inches is that?

Write a sentence comparing the python to a real thing of about the same length.
(For example: The longest python is about the same length as five Michaels lying end to end.)

**1.** Estimate the shaded part of each figure using $\frac{2}{3}$, $\frac{1}{2}$, and $\frac{3}{4}$.

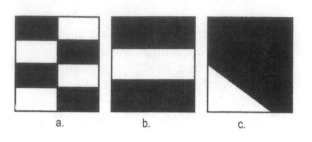

a.        b.        c.

**2.** Compare each pair of fractions.

**a.** $\frac{5}{7}$ ☐ $\frac{4}{6}$

**b.** $\frac{2}{3}$ ☐ $\frac{24}{36}$

**c.** $\frac{8}{9}$ ☐ $\frac{9}{8}$

**3.** Solve for x.  **0.4x = 1**

**4.** Solve for c.  **75 = 15c**

## 5. Challenge Problem

Pythons have beautiful skin patterns. Make a pattern on the snake's back. Describe your pattern.

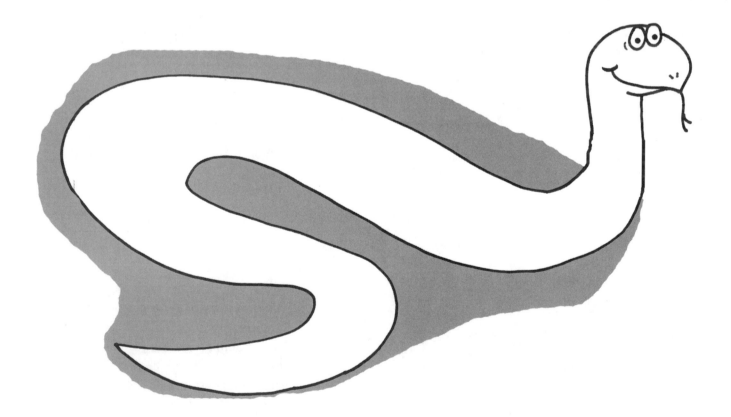

1. In the USA, around 350 million pairs of sports shoes are bought every year. Write the number as a multiple of a power of ten.

More power to you.

2. Which of the following operations would you use to isolate the variable in $y - 2 = 16$?

    a. Add 16 to both sides.

    b. Subtract 16 from both sides.

    c. Add two to both sides.

    d. Subtract two from both sides.

3. Insert operation symbols to make the statement true.

    (12 ___ 8) ___ (5 ___ 2) = 11

4. Use mental math to find the product.

    **1,000 x 9,002 = _____**

5. Rubber soles on athletic shoes made the shoes less noisy, so wearers could sneak around. The term "sneaker" was first used in 1916 by the US Rubber Company for Keds. Do you have enough information to determine how many months ago that was?

The years really "sneak" up on you.

Calendar

1. Solve the equation.

    **0.8p = 32**

2. When you run, your feet hit the ground around 800 times every mile. Estimate how many times your feet would hit the ground in a 26-mile marathon.

After a 26-mile run, I get a little slap-happy.

3. Which operation would you perform first in each expression?

    **a. (6.4 – 3.2) x 10**

    **b. 0.3 x 10 ÷ 3 –1**

4. Write the fourth term of the number pattern.

    **1, 0.2, 0.04, _____**

5. What is the average price for Corkers Wading Shoes?

    **Corkers Studded
    Rubber-Soled Waders** . . . . $34.95

    **Corkers Studded
    Felt-Soled Waders** . . . . . . $45.95

    **Corkers Convertible
    Studded Shoes** . . . . . . . . $69.99

    **Corkers sandals** . . . . . . . $49.99

    **Corkers Convertible
    High-Rise** . . . . . . . . . . . $129.99

1. Alice has three pairs of athletic shoes. She randomly chooses one shoe. Then, she randomly chooses a second shoe. Are the chances that she will pick a second shoe that matches the first the same as the chance of picking a particular shoe on the first pick? Explain.

2. Use an integer to represent each situation.
   a. a bank deposit of $35.00
   b. 17° C below zero
   c. a debt of $7.00

3. Simplify the expression.

   $$[3 + (-5)] \times [(-2) - (-4)] \div (-2)$$

4. The National Sports Goods Association reports that $13 billion was spent on athletic shoes and sports footwear. If the average pair of athletic shoes cost $50.00, how many pairs does the $13 billion total represent?

5. Peter asked 49 sixth graders what size shoe they wore. He recorded his findings in this table. What is the average shoe size of the 49 students Peter surveyed? (Round the average to the nearest size.)

| SHOE SIZE | NUMBER OF STUDENTS |
|-----------|--------------------|
| 6 | II |
| 7 | ᴎᴎ |
| 8 | ᴎᴎ  ᴎᴎ  IIII |
| 9 | ᴎᴎ ᴎᴎ ᴎᴎ ᴎᴎ ᴎᴎ |
| 10 | III |

1. In the past 13 years, over 13 million pairs of athletic shoes have been recycled. The shoes are ground down to become sports courts, tracks, and playing surfaces. If the rate of recycling doubles, how many pairs of shoes will be recycled in a year? (Assume that the same number of shoes was recycled each of the 13 years.)

2. Do the ratios form a proportion?
   a. $\frac{8}{5}, \frac{11}{7}$
   b. $\frac{36}{72}, \frac{27}{54}$

3. What is the regular price of a pair of athletic shoes that costs $36.00 during a 20% off sale?

4. Solve the problem. **8,945 + 43,219 + 6,234**

5. About how long is each shoelace?

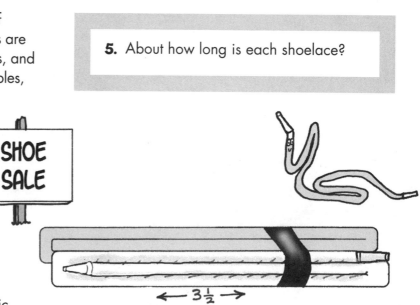

$\leftarrow 3\frac{1}{2} \rightarrow$

**1.** Solve the equation. $\frac{a}{4} = 11$

**2.** Draw the next design in the pattern.

**3.** What is **82 percent of 200**?

**4.** Match the description of the sides to the name of the triangle.

three congruent sides •     • scalene triangle

at least two congruent sides •     • equilateral triangle

no congruent sides •     • isosceles triangle

**Order Form**

| Qty: | Item # | Item Description | Unit Price | Total Price |
|------|--------|------------------|------------|-------------|
| ____ | 3-808910 | Speed Trainer size____ | $64.99 | ____ |
| ____ | 3-253150 | Beanie | $18.00 | ____ |

Free Shipping - UPS Ground with orders of $48.00 or more.
2nd Day UPS $9.95

Subtotal: ____
6% Sales Tax: ____
Shipping: ____
Gift Certificate: ____
Merchandise Order: ____

Happy Birthday Traci!

*Gift Certificate*
Amount: Fifty dollars
To: Traci Green
Certificate to be used before Dec. 2010

love, Grandma

## 5. Challenge Problem

Traci has a $50.00 gift card for Sports Specialty. She has decided to buy some shoes and a beanie. She wants the order shipped UPS second day. Complete the form for the order. Calculate the sales tax and shipping costs. Subtract the amount of the gift card. How much will Traci need to pay? How much would Traci save if she had the order shipped UPS Ground?

1. Hawaii's total area is 10,932 square miles. Its land area is equal to 6,423 square miles. Round the numbers to the nearest 100.

   a. About what is Hawaii's total water area?

   b. About what percent of its total area is water?

2. The last census reported Hawaii's population as 1,211,537. Write an equation to find the population per square mile. (Use the land area figure in problem one.)

3. Write each number in standard form and in words.

   **a. 7,000,000 + 49,000 + 4**

   **b. 500,000 + 3,000 + 500 +2**

4. Solve the problem.

   **89,500 – 30,714 =**

5. Sheila will make a flower lei. She has red flowers, purple flowers, and white flowers. She will choose the flowers randomly from a basket. Use a tree diagram to figure out the possibilities for the first three flowers. How many possibilities are there?

1. The population of Hawaii grew 9.3 percent from the 1990 census to the 2000 census. It is estimated that the population will grow only 4.2 percent from 2000 to 2010. What is the difference in the population growth?

2. What is the square root of 25?

3. Solve the problem.

   **290.4 ÷ 8 =**

   (Round your answer to the nearest hundredth.)

4. Solve the equation.

   **0.6x = 30**

5. Choose an appropriate unit for each measurement.

   a. weight of one pineapple

   b. weight of a handful of macadamia nuts

   c. length of a surfboard

   d. capacity of a swimming pool

Ah, surfing!

1. A whole number is divisible by two it if ends in
   ○ 2 or 4
   ○ 6 or 8
   ○ 0
   ○ any of the digits 2, 4, 6, 8, or 0

2. Write the expression using exponents.

   **2 x 2 x 2 x 2 x 2 x 2 x 6 x 6**

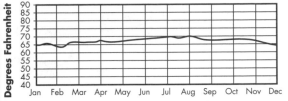
This is my favorite vacation spot.

3. Which expression has a sum of −8?
   a. − 12 + ( −4)
   b. − 11 + 3
   c. − 5 + 3
   d. 9 + ( −1)

The temperature here is always perfect.

4. Write a subtraction problem involving a positive integer and a negative integer with a positive answer.

5. The line graph shows the daily mean temperature in Kahului, Hawaii. Temperatures from 30 years were used to determine the means.

Degrees Fahrenheit
90 85 80 75 70 65 60 55 50 45 40
Jan Feb Mar Apr May Jun Jul Aug Sep Oct Nov Dec

a. What is the difference between the highest mean temperature and the lowest mean temperature?

b. In what months did the highest mean temperature occur?

c. What observation can you make about temperature fluctuations in Kahului?

1. Label each pair of shapes as **similar, congruent, neither similar** or **congruent.**

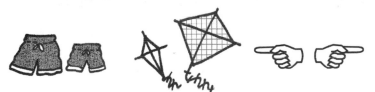

2. Solve the problem.

   $$2\frac{1}{2} + 3\frac{1}{4} =$$

3. Solve for x.

   $$x + \frac{2}{3} = \frac{8}{15}$$

4. Keli loves taking long walks on the beach. Estimate the time of her stroll. She began walking at 4:27 p.m. and finished at 8:15 p.m.

5. Mauna Kea is the tallest volcano on the Island of Hawaii. From sea floor to summit it towers more than 5.6 miles (9 km). If the summit of Mauna Kea is 13,796 feet above sea level, draw a diagram to show how much of Mauna Kea lies below sea level.

I have deep roots.

Compare the populations.

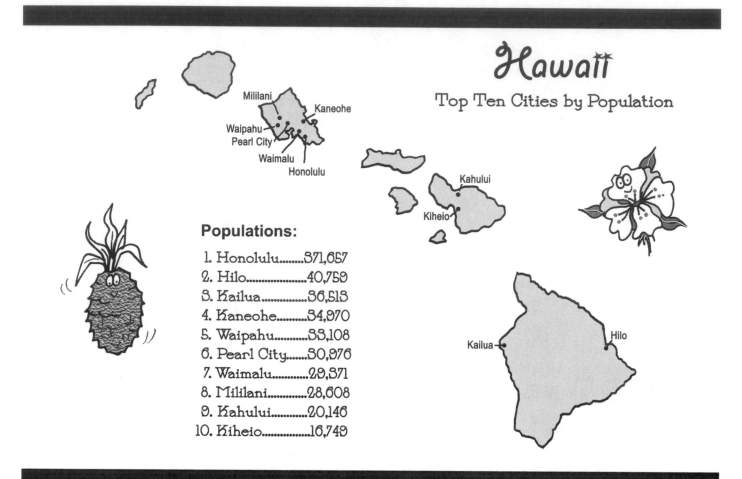

**Hawaii**

Top Ten Cities by Population

Mililani

Kaneohe

Waipahu
Pearl City

Waimalu

Honolulu

Kahului

Kiheio

Kailua

Hilo

**Populations:**

1. Honolulu.........371,657
2. Hilo....................40,759
3. Kailua...............36,513
4. Kaneohe...........34,970
5. Waipahu............33,108
6. Pearl City.......30,976
7. Waimalu............29,371
8. Mililani............28,608
9. Kahului...........20,146
10. Kiheio..............16,749

**1.** How many more people live in Honolulu than Waipahu?

**2.** What statement can you make about the population of Honolulu compared with the other nine cities?

**3.** About how many more people live in Honolulu than Hilo and Pearl City?

**4.** What statement can you make about the population of Kailua compared with the population of Kihei?

**5.** What type of graph would be a good one to use to show the information on the table?

**1.** A mountain climber scaled both Mt. Aconcagua (6,960 meters) and Mt. Kilimanjaro (5,895 meters). How many meters did she climb?

**2.** Altitude sickness is a problem for climbers who climb to elevations above 12,000 feet. Would climbing Mt. Aconcagua or Mt. Kilimanjaro pose an altitude sickness problem?

**3.** Test each number for divisibility by 9.
   a. 1,186
   b. 3,807
   c. 978
   d. 738

Which one of these numbers has nine lives?

**4.** The success ratio for amateur climbers trying to climb Mt. Everest is 1 in 4. If you join a party of 16 climbers, what is the probability that you will be successful in making it to the summit?

**5.** Estimate the surface area of the face of Mt. Magma shown on the graph.

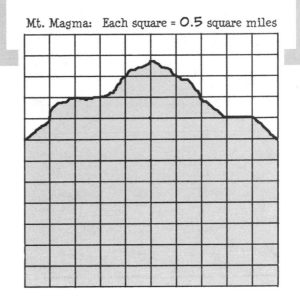

Mt. Magma: Each square = 0.5 square miles

**1.** Mt. Kilimanjaro is 40 times as tall as the Great Pyramid in Egypt. Mt. Kilimanjaro is 5,895 meters high. About how tall is the Great Pyramid? Write a sentence that compares a mountain peak with your school building.

**2.** Which statement represents the **Commutative Property of Addition?**
   a. 6 + 3 = 9      b. 7 + 2 = 8 + 1
   c. 4 + 5 = 5 + 4    d. 9 + 0 = 9

**3.** Solve the problem. (Round your answer to the nearest hundredth.)

   **9.54 ÷ 2.6 =**

**4.** Solve for p.

   **2p + 1.3 = 3**

We're climbing shoes.

**5.** Henry needs new climbing shoes. His grandmother has given him a gift certificate for $200.00. Choose a pair of shoes and additional climbing gear for Henry to buy with his gift certificate. The total should be within $5 of $200.00.

| | |
|---|---|
| Ascenders and Descenders | $26.95 |
| Beanie | $9.80 |
| Carbiners | |
|     Locking | $19.00 |
|     Non-locking | $7.50 |
| Harnesses | $29.95 |
| Helmet | $69.95 |
| Pullover | $79.00 |
| Shirt | $42.00 |
| Sporting Rock Shoes | $75.00 |
| Mad Rock Shoes | $59.00 |
| Monkey Rock Shoes | $39.00 |

1. Many Sherpas act as guides on Mt. Everest. If a Sherpa has guided 15 groups of climbers from a base camp at 5,486 meters to the summit of Mt. Everest (8,850 meters), how many kilometers of vertical elevation has he traveled as a guide?

2. Compare using **<** or **>**.

   a.  3  ☐  – 13

   b.  –7  ☐  – 6

   c.  –8  ☐  0

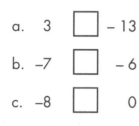

Heights make me dizzy.

3. Solve the problem.

   $$\frac{m}{5} = -4$$

4. Name a triangle with sides 8, 9, and 8.

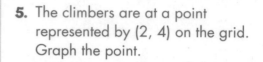

5. The climbers are at a point represented by (2, 4) on the grid. Graph the point.

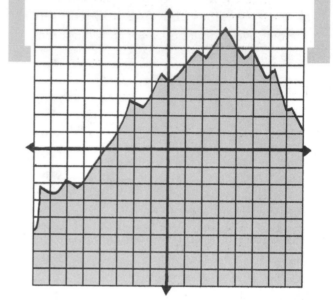

1. Mont Blanc, in the European Alps, is 4,810 meters. A climber can cover 200 vertical feet per hour. Is it reasonable to imagine that the climber's party will complete the hike in 24 hours? How many hours will it take to reach the summit?

2. A mountain climber signed up to climb Cho Oyu, an 8,000-meter peak. The cost of the climb is $20,000.00 and requires six weeks. What is the cost per meter climbed?

3. Find the number of possible permutations of the letters **P, E, A, K**.

4. If the map scale is 1 cm = 100 km, estimate the actual distance between two camps that are 5 cm apart on the map.

5. If you multiply a number by six and then subtract five, the result is 13. What is the number?

Maybe we'll find the missing number on the other side.

### Highest Peak on Each Continent

| Continent | Highest Peak | Height in feet (to the nearest 100 ft) | Height in meters |
|---|---|---|---|
| Africa | Kilimanjaro | 19,300 | _____ |
| Antarctica | Vinson Massif | 16,100 | _____ |
| Asia | Everest | 29,005 | _____ |
| Australia | Kosciusko | 7,300 | _____ |
| Europe | Elbrus | 18,500 | _____ |
| North America | McKinley | 20,300 | _____ |
| South America | Aconcagua | 22,800 | _____ |

Complete the chart by converting the elevations in feet to meters. Round the heights to the nearest 10 m.

**1.** What is the range in feet of the highest peaks?

**2.** Find the mean and median heights in meters of the highest peaks.

Pop, will I ever grow as tall as you?

Just wait a few million years, son.

**3.** Which peaks are taller than the mean?

**4.** Which peaks are taller than the median?

## 5. Challenge Problem

Why aren't the answers to problems three and four the same?

**1.** Circle the common multiples of four and three.

**24**    **34**    **76**

**2.** The pet store has 20 mice: 11 are white, five are grey, and four are brown. If the pet storeowner randomly chooses a mouse for the window display, what is the probability that the mouse will be grey?

**3.** Solve for z.

**3z + 22 − z = 162**

**4.** What is the value of the digit **7** in the number **846,723,100**?

**5.** Pet mice exercise by running on an exercise wheel. If the wheel is six inches in diameter, how far does the mouse run each time the wheel makes one complete circle? Round your answer to the nearest half-inch. How many times would the wheel have to turn before the mouse ran one yard?

Is this what they mean by the "rat race"?

**1.** Which unit would be best to measure the food in the mouse's dish?

   a. ounces

   b. pounds

   c. tons

What do you think I am, a bath tub?

DISH

**2.** Whiskers always eats 75 percent of the food he shares with Twitch. If the food bowl holds two ounces of food, how much does Whiskers eat?

**3.** Order the set of decimals as they would appear on a number line.

**9.2, 9.28, 9.13, 9.25, 9.26**

**4.** Solve the problem.

**38.27 ÷ 43 =**

**5.** Harriet wants to buy two pet mice, a cage, food, and a water bottle. She earned $20.00 babysitting for her neighbors. Does she have enough to make the purchase? Figure out the answer using mental math.

*Big Sale*
Mice - $3.25 each
Basic cage + free bedding
$12.00
Water bottles
$2.00

1. What is the absolute value?

    a. –3

    b. 16

    c. –1

    d. 0

2. Find the sum.

    **89 + (–176) =**

3. You flip a coin six times. Find the probability of getting three tails.

4. True or false?

    **Perpendicular lines are always parallel.**

5. Find the multiples of four to help the mouse get through the maze.

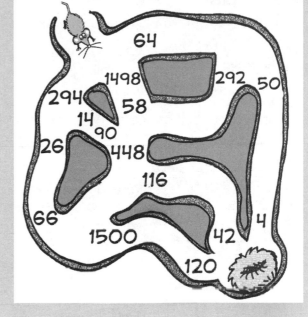

64

1498    292    50

294    58

14

90

26    448

116

66

1500    42    4

120

1. Find the value of **g** if **c = 17**.

    **41 = c + 2g – 100**

2. Write each fraction as a decimal and a percent.

    a. $\frac{3}{5}$ _____  _____

    b. $\frac{3}{4}$ _____  _____

    c. $\frac{1}{2}$ _____  _____

3. Solve for **t**.

    $\frac{1}{3}t = 333$

4. True or false?

    **The Associative Property of Multiplication states that changing the grouping of factors does not change the product.**

5. The average life span of a mouse is $1\frac{1}{2}$ years. Choose the range that is closest to that number.

    ○ 365 – 457 days

    ○ 8,760 –13,152 hours

    ○ 525,600 – 650,000 minutes

Squeak, squeak!

- Baby mice are called pinkies. They are deaf, naked, and blind at birth.
- After two weeks the babies look just like their parents.
- An average white-footed mouse mother has ten litters per year.
- An average litter is five babies.

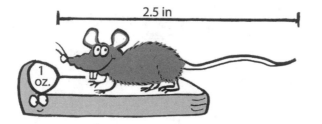

2.5 in

1 OZ.

For these problems, assume that two out of every three babies in a litter is female and that young females have their first litters at 16 weeks.

**1.** How many mice would it take to balance the weight of a half-pound chunk of cheese?

**2.** If a mouse's tail is one and a half times the length of its body, how long is the tail of a mouse measuring two and one-half inches?

**3.** Write an equation to find the number of feet 15 mice have. Solve it.

**4.** Write an equation to find the number of whiskers if the average mouse has 15 on each side of its nose. Solve it.

# 5. Challenge Problem

Choose the number of mother mice with babies at the end of one year.

○ only one          ○ less than 25          ○ less than 40          ○ more than 50

Explain your reasoning.

What implications would this problem have for a grain farmer who finds a nest of baby mice in his storage bin in January?

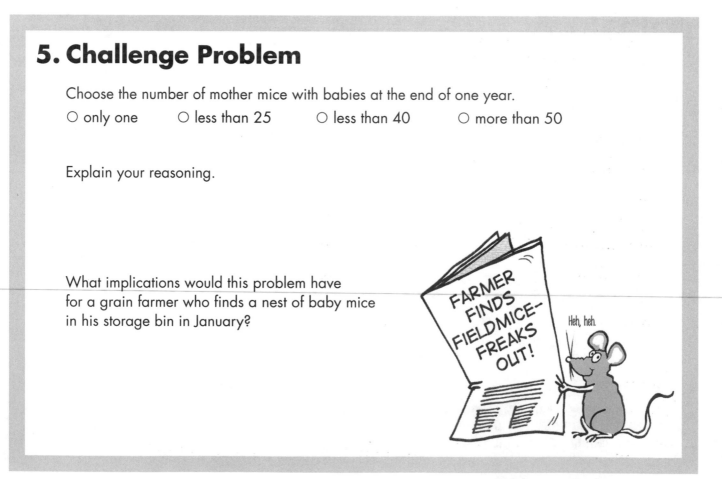

FARMER FINDS FIELDMICE- FREAKS OUT!

Heh, heh.

**1.** Excavation for the Empire State Building began on January 22, 1930. Construction began on March 17, 1930. How many days were in the excavation phase of construction? (1930 was not a leap year.)

**2.** The Empire State Building has over 10 million bricks. Write that number in scientific notation.

**3.** There are 5,476 high-rise buildings in NYC. Currently 108 new high-rises are under construction, and 29 more have been approved for construction. How many high-rises will NYC have when all of those approved buildings are constructed?

**4.** Solve the problem.

**85,692 x 294 =**

**5.** Name the figures.

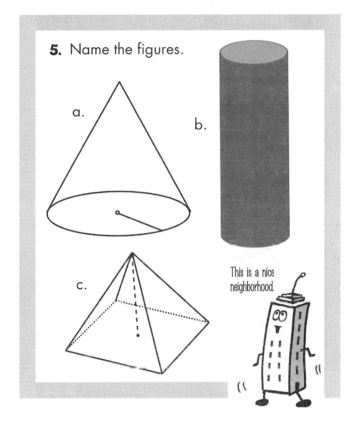

a.

b.

c.

This is a nice neighborhood.

**1.** Ben got on the subway at 11:20 a.m. He arrived at the museum at 12:13 p.m. How long was the ride?

Don't be late.

**2.** Solve the problem.

**8.56 x 9.863 =**

**3.** A hot-dog vendor received $20.00 for a $4.25 purchase. Is the vendor most likely to use estimation, mental math, paper and pencil, or a calculator to determine the amount of change? Why?

**4.** Use **<**, **=**, or **>** to complete the statement.

**2,643.02 + 4, 827.038 _____ 747.0058**

**5.** Tanisha will take the AirTrain from Jay Steet to JFK Airport. She has a MetroCard with $4 credit. Her subway ride will cost $2, and the AirTrain ticket will cost $5. She will get on the subway at Jay St. station and go to Howard Beach to catch the AirTrain. How much money will she need to add to her card to cover the cost for the subway and the AirTrain?

It's only money.

**1.** Find each product.

a. –3 x 5

b. –16 x 4

c. –32 x (–17)

Work it out.

**2.** Tony buys an apple from the street vendor. The vendor reaches into the barrel and pulls one out. If two-thirds of the apples are red and one-third are green, what is the chance of Tony getting a green apple?

**3.** What is the circumference of the circle?

$c = \pi d$

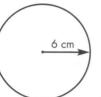
6 cm

**4.** A carton is three feet square. What is its volume?

**5.** Here is the fare schedule for the Long Island Bus.

| Cash Fare | Adult | Senior/ Disabled | Student with ID |
|---|---|---|---|
| One-way | $2.00 | $1.00 | $1.80 |
| One-way with transfer | $2.25 | $1.10 | $2.05 |

a. What percent of the fare does a senior citizen save by purchasing a senior ticket rather than an adult ticket?

b. What is the cost of four adult round trips with transfers?

**1.** Write the mixed numbers as improper fractions.

a. $3\frac{3}{4}$          c. $2\frac{7}{8}$

b. $8\frac{1}{2}$          d. $4\frac{3}{5}$

Can you do the math?

**2.** Find the sum or difference.

a. $\frac{1}{3} + \frac{4}{5} =$

b. $\frac{3}{4} - \frac{7}{10} =$

**3.** Use mental math. What is $\frac{4}{5}$ of 2,500? Explain the steps you went through to get the answer.

**4.** The Empire State Building has 6,400 windows. If there were the same number of windows on each of the 102 floors, how many windows would be on each floor?

**5.** Measure the souvenir. Record the length of each side to the nearest cm.

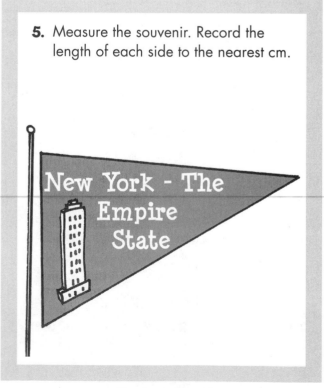
New York - The Empire State

Each building is drawn to scale by height. The diagram sorts the structures by height without considering their antennas.

1. What is the median height of the buildings on the graph?

2. What is the range of the heights?

3. How many buildings are within ten meters of the median? Name them.

4. What two buildings are rectangular prisms?

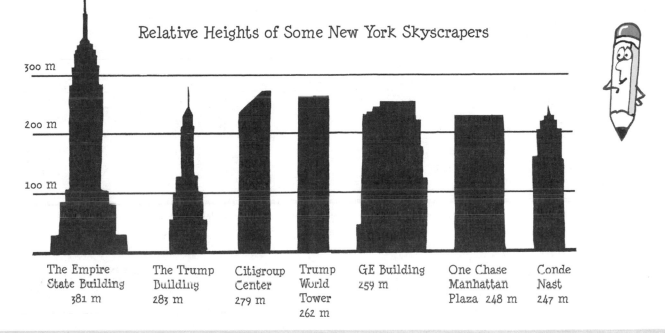

Relative Heights of Some New York Skyscrapers

300 m

200 m

100 m

The Empire State Building 381 m

The Trump Building 283 m

Citigroup Center 279 m

Trump World Tower 262 m

GE Building 259 m

One Chase Manhattan Plaza 248 m

Conde Nast 247 m

## 5. Challenge Problem

Look at the table showing the ten tallest buildings in the world. Write several sentences comparing the size of the Empire State Building to another building on the table.

| Building | City | Height | Height | Floors | Year Built |
|---|---|---|---|---|---|
| Taipei 101 | Taipei | 509 m | 1,671 ft | 101 | 2004 |
| Petronas Tower 1 | Kuala Lumpur | 452 m | 1,483 ft | 88 | 1998 |
| Petronas Tower 2 | Kuala Lumpur | 452 m | 1,483 ft | 88 | 1998 |
| Sears Tower | Chicago | 442 m | 1,451 ft | 108 | 1974 |
| Jin Mao Tower | Shanghai | 421 m | 1,380 ft | 88 | 1998 |
| Two International Finance | Hong Kong | 415 m | 1,362 ft | 88 | 2003 |
| CITIC Plaza | Guangzhou | 391 m | 1,260 ft | 80 | 1997 |
| Shun Hing Square | Shenzhen | 384 m | 1,250 ft | 69 | 1996 |
| Empire State Building | New York City | 381 m | 1,250 ft | 102 | 1931 |
| Central Plaza | Hong Kong | 374 m | 1,227 ft | 78 | 1992 |

**1.** The diameter of the Earth at the equator is about 7,900 miles. What is a good estimate of the circumference of the Earth?

**2.** Fill in the missing sign for each problem.

   **a.** 28,000 _____ 140 = 200

   **b.** 8,963 _____ 255 = 8,708

   **c.** 500 _____ 60 = 30,000

   **d.** 69,500 _____ 1,500 = 71,000

**3.** Estimate the size of this angle.

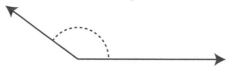

**4.** Choose the greatest common factor of 36 and 60.

   ○ 6       ○ 3       ○ 12

**5.** Earth is about 248,550 miles from the moon and 93,000,000 from the sun. What is the difference in the distances? What observation can you make about the relative didifference between the distance from earth to the moon and the distance from earth to the sun?

I think you're just going through a phase.

**1.** A lake has a surface of 35,000 square feet. Thirty-five percent of the lake is in the sun. How many square feet of the lake are not in the sun?

**2.** Mandy scored 85 percent on the earth science test. If there were 60 problems and each problem was worth two points, how many problems did Mandy miss?

**3.** A kilometer is closest to

   ○ a meter       ○ an acre

   ○ a mile        ○ a centimeter

   ○ a yard

**4.** Write a decimal for each percentage.

   a. 35% _____

   b. 350% _____

   c. 3.5% _____

   d. 0.35% _____

**5.** Continue the patterns on the signs.

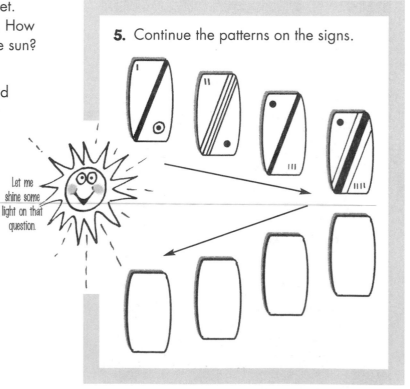

Let me shine some light on that question.

1. Define the term **congruent**.

2. The Earth travels through space at 67,000 miles per hour. How many miles does the Earth travel in a day? Write your answer in standard notation and in scientific notation.

3. Simplify the equation. **6(–3p + 8) = 120**

4. The temperature on Friday was –18.5° F. This was five times colder than Sunday's temperature. What was the temperature on Sunday?

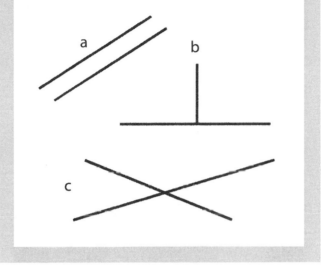

Brrr! What is the temperature?

5. a. Which pair(s) of line segments intersects?

   b. Which pair is perpendicular?

   c. Which pair is parallel?

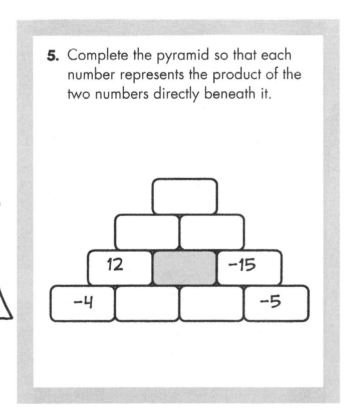

1. The mean surface temperature on earth is 15° C. Explain what that means. How does the mean temperature compare with the temperature at your location today?

2. The Earth's distance from the sun changes depending on its place in orbit, but the mean distance from the sun is 149,600,000 km. Round the number to the nearest ten million km.

3. Circle the fractions that are equivalent to $\frac{6}{15}$.

$\frac{1}{5}$    $\frac{3}{5}$    $\frac{9}{30}$

$\frac{18}{45}$    $\frac{2}{5}$    $\frac{12}{30}$

Circle it.

4. The answer to the problem is $\frac{2}{3}$. What is the problem?

   a. $\frac{2}{3} - \left(-\frac{1}{2}\right) =$    c. $\frac{4}{9} - \frac{4}{6} =$

   b. $\frac{5}{8} \times \frac{2}{3} =$    d. none of the above

5. Complete the pyramid so that each number represents the product of the two numbers directly beneath it.

**1.** The Earth's atmosphere is a thin layer of gases that surrounds the Earth. It is about 300 miles thick, but 80 percent of the atmosphere is within ten miles of the surface of the earth. What can you infer about the 20 percent of the atmosphere that represents the remaining 290 miles?

**2.** Which gas is found in greatest quantities in the atmosphere?

**3.** Four NASA space shuttles flew through the atmosphere on 19 missions from 1999 to 2002. What kind of graph would be appropriate to show how many different missions each of the four space shuttles flew?

**4.** Draw a graph for the following data:
Atlantis, six missions; Columbia, two missions; Discovery, five missions; Endeavour, six missions.

### Elements in Earth's Atmosphere

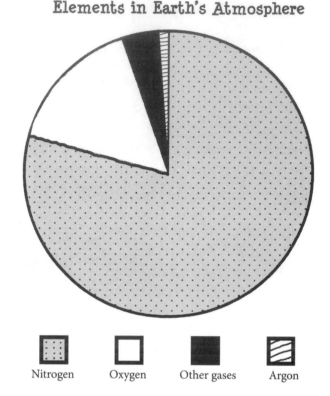

Nitrogen    Oxygen    Other gases    Argon

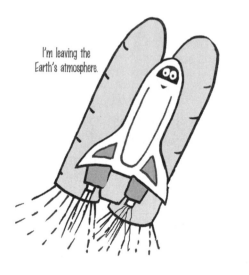

I'm leaving the Earth's atmosphere.

## 5. Challenge Problem

Imagine that you are looking at your graph for the first time. What information on the graph seems most important?

1. Write the number in words. **84,706,003**

2. Find the value of the expression.

   **(16 + 32) ÷ 12**

3. Write the next three terms and the rule for the number pattern.

   **2, 6, 18, 54, _____, _____, _____**

4. Circle and name the triangle that has three equal sides.

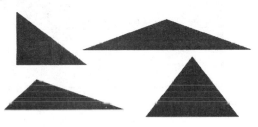

5. Claire asked twenty customers to name their favorite bakery treat. Group the responses in categories, then make a line plot to show the data. What conclusion can you draw from the data?

*Doughnuts!*  *Muffins!*

| | |
|---|---|
| glazed doughnut | German chocolate cake |
| sugar cookie | angel food cake |
| chocolate cake | frosted cookie |
| chocolate chip cookie | cupcakes |
| bear's claw | peanut butter cookie |
| oatmeal cookie | brownies |
| chocolate doughnut | apple pie |
| banana nut muffin | chocolate muffin |
| apple turnover | doughnut holes |
| chocolate chip cookie | double-chocolate cake |

1. The four servers at the bakery equally share $87.44 in tips. How much does each server receive?

2. Solve the problem.

   **144 + 56 ÷ 4**

3. Write the equality shown on the number line below.

4. If the bakery charges $1.76 for a 16-ounce baguette and $2.20 for a 20-ounce baguette, what will probably be the charge for a 24-ounce baguette?

5. Draw a cookie bar. It must be a rectangular prism measuring 2" long and 1" tall.

*Does it have raisins?*

**1.** Peri buys a sack of doughnut holes with ten glazed and ten chocolate. Are the chances of randomly choosing two of the same kind in a row better or worse than choosing two different kinds of in a row?

**2.** Solve the equation.

$$-4 + \frac{h}{4} = 4$$

**3.** Mom has $30 in her purse. She puts in $12 and spends $33. How much money does she have now?

**4.** True or false?

**A positive integer minus a negative integer is always a negative integer.**

**5.** Find the surface area of the cake.

Sitting on a birthday cake is my favorite job.

6 in

7 in

**1.** Dan bought a loaf of bread for $2.10 and cookies for $.50 each. He spent a total of $6.60. How many cookies did he buy? Write an equation and then solve it.

**2.** Solve for x.

$$x + 6\frac{4}{9} = 8\frac{1}{9}$$

**3.** Write each fraction in its simplest form.

　a. $\frac{40}{50}$

　b. $\frac{24}{60}$

　c. $\frac{14}{84}$

**4.** Which measurement is most reasonable?
　○ The cookie weighs $\frac{1}{2}$ pound.
　○ The cake weighs 32 ounces.
　○ The pie weighs one gram.

**5.** All the pies at a bakery are the same size. Cherry pies are cut into eight equal pieces. Cream pies are cut into six equal pieces. Two slices of cherry pie and three slices of cream pie are placed in a pie tin for a carryout order. What fraction of the pie tin is filled?

Yum!

Fill my pie order, please.

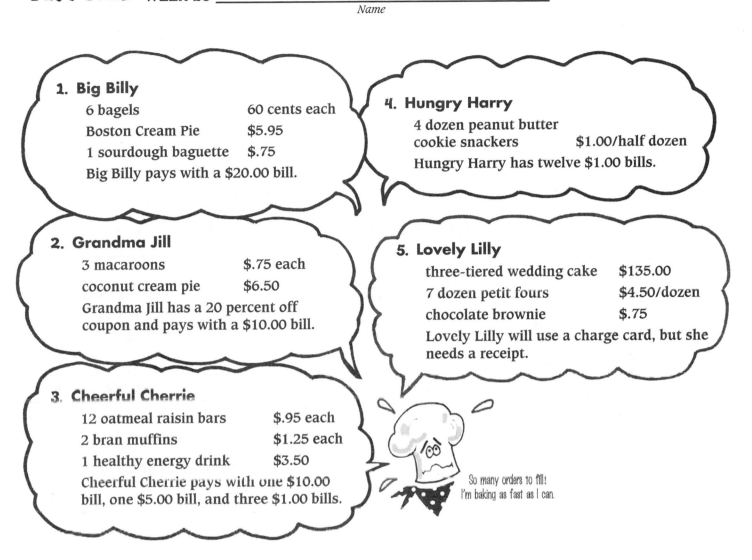

**1. Big Billy**

| | |
|---|---|
| 6 bagels | 60 cents each |
| Boston Cream Pie | $5.95 |
| 1 sourdough baguette | $.75 |

Big Billy pays with a $20.00 bill.

**2. Grandma Jill**

| | |
|---|---|
| 3 macaroons | $.75 each |
| coconut cream pie | $6.50 |

Grandma Jill has a 20 percent off coupon and pays with a $10.00 bill.

**3. Cheerful Cherrie**

| | |
|---|---|
| 12 oatmeal raisin bars | $.95 each |
| 2 bran muffins | $1.25 each |
| 1 healthy energy drink | $3.50 |

Cheerful Cherrie pays with one $10.00 bill, one $5.00 bill, and three $1.00 bills.

**4. Hungry Harry**

| | |
|---|---|
| 4 dozen peanut butter cookie snackers | $1.00/half dozen |

Hungry Harry has twelve $1.00 bills.

**5. Lovely Lilly**

| | |
|---|---|
| three-tiered wedding cake | $135.00 |
| 7 dozen petit fours | $4.50/dozen |
| chocolate brownie | $.75 |

Lovely Lilly will use a charge card, but she needs a receipt.

*So many orders to fill! I'm baking as fast as I can.*

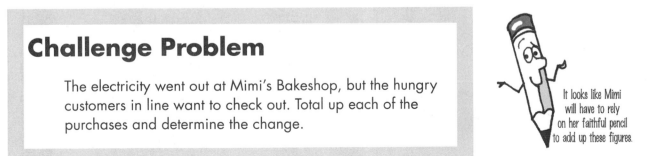

## Challenge Problem

The electricity went out at Mimi's Bakeshop, but the hungry customers in line want to check out. Total up each of the purchases and determine the change.

*It looks like Mimi will have to rely on her faithful pencil to add up these figures.*

**1.** There are more than 60 million pet dogs in the U.S., and nearly 70 million pet cats. Write each number in scientific notation and use your numbers to determine the sum.

**2.** Is the dog bone symmetrical? If so, how many lines of symmetry can be drawn?

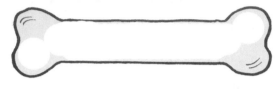

**3.** The Centers for Disease Control and Prevention reports that dog bites send nearly 368,000 victims to hospital emergency departments per year. About how many bites is that per day?

**4.** Check each number for divisibility by three.

a. **2,685**  b. **981**  c. **328**

**5.** How many different combinations of doggie treat bags can you make if each bag contains two items, and you choose one from Group A and one from Group B?

| Group A | Group B |
| --- | --- |
| crunchy nugget | mini-bone |
| cheese chew | bacon biscuit |
| tasty tart | doggie cookie |

**1.** Households with dogs spent 38 percent more on veterinary care in 2001 than they did in 1996. If the Sutters spent $120.00 in 1996, estimate how much they spent in 2001.

**2.** What percent of the total pet dog and cat population includes pet dogs?

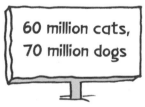

60 million cats, 70 million dogs

**3.** Use the Distributive Property to simplify the expression.

**3 x 19**

**4.** Carla's puppy was 28" tall, and Gwen's pup was only 14" tall. Each puppy doubled its size. How much taller is Carla's pup than Gwen's pup?

**5.** The organization, Guide Dogs of America, reports that 70 percent of its guide dogs are Labrador retrievers, 15 percent are golden retrievers, and 15 percent are German shepherds. If dogs were assigned randomly, what is the chance of receiving a golden retriever?

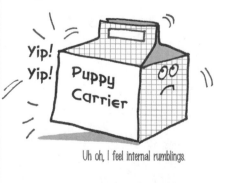

Yip! Yip! Puppy Carrier

Uh oh, I feel internal rumblings.

1. The average dog visits the veterinarian about twice as often as the average horse. Write a formula to find the number of times Pat takes her dog to the vet. She takes her horse to the vet twice a year.

2. Order from the least to the greatest.

   **– 6, 8, 7, –8**

3. **–54 ÷ 6**

4. Scott and his dog Mackenzie like to play ball. Scott has to be home for supper at 6 p.m. He gets home from school at 4:30 p.m. If it takes 20 minutes to walk to the park, how long will the two have for a game? (Don't forget they will have to walk home from the park, too.)

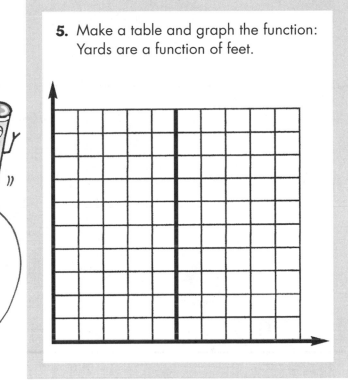

5. Make a table and graph the function: Yards are a function of feet.

1. Find each quotient. Express your answers in the lowest terms.

   a. $1\frac{1}{3}$ of $\frac{1}{5}$    b. $\frac{8}{9}$ of $\frac{2}{3}$    c. $\frac{7}{8} \times \frac{3}{4}$

2. Choose an appropriate unit for the capacity of the dog's water dish.

   a. gallons        c. pounds
   b. ounces         d. pints

3. Write an equation to solve the problem. Then solve it.

   **Sam's Pet Shop has 45 animals. If the number of animals for sale increased by eight percent, how many animals would there be?**

4. Pet owners reclaim about 650,000 dogs and cats from shelters each year. This number represents 35 percent of the number of dogs and cats entering shelters. How many dogs and cats enter shelters every year?

5. Find the area of the dog pen.

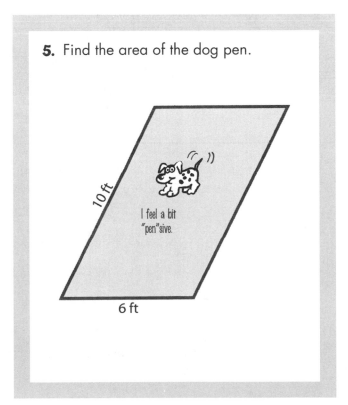

10 ft

I feel a bit "pen"sive.

6 ft

Pet Snax keeps a table showing their expenses and income every month.
Use the table to figure the company's profit or loss.

## PET SNAX, INC.
### 1600 PEDIGREE PLAZA, DOGVILLE, U.S.A.
### E-MAIL: SNAX@CANINE.PAWZ

**MEMO**

I need help with the books.

Leave a memo.

| Pet Snax | | |
|---|---|---|
| **Month** | **Income** | **Expenses** |
| January | $7, 648 | –$5,025 |
| February | $8,328 | –$5,227 |
| March | $7,394 | –$6,782 |
| April | $7,541 | –$7,649 |
| May | $7,302 | –$7,497 |
| June | $8,274 | –$6,538 |

**1.** Explain how you would find out whether Pet Snax made a profit or loss.

**2.** Put a plus by each month in which the company made a profit, and a minus by each month in which the company showed a loss.

**3.** Did the company have a profit during this six-month period? If so, what was it?

**4.** What was the average income per month?

**5.** What was the average expense?

1. Tristan flew from Los Angeles to Boston. Boston is three hours ahead of L.A. Tristan's flight took four hours and 35 minutes, and Tristan left L.A. at 9:45 a.m. What time did he arrive in Boston?

2. Choose the greatest common factor of 16 and 48.

   ○ 4          ○ 8          ○ 16

3. Find the value of **x**.

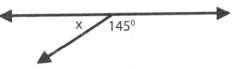

4. Josh's cuckoo clock cuckoos once on each quarter hour. How many times will it cuckoo from 1:15 p.m. to 8:00 p.m.? Explain the strategy you used to solve the problem.

5. A spinner is divided into three equal sections colored red, blue, and yellow. What is the probability of spinning red and then yellow?

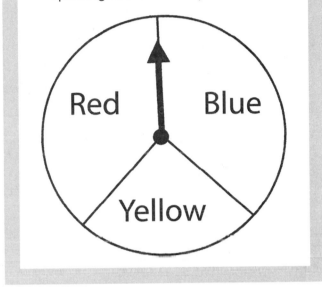

1. Which units are used to measure time?

   a. minutes and seconds
   b. hours and acres
   c. days and tons

2. Solve the problem.

   **396 ÷ 8.8 =**

3. Ken bought a new alarm clock for $16.95. He paid 30 percent less than the original price. What was the original price of the clock?

4. What property is represented by the equation?

   **5 + 7 = 7 + 5**

Hmmm, let me check the time.

5. How long is the minute hand? Give your answer to the nearest quarter-inch.

**1.** For every 200 watches, ten are defective. How many defective watches would you expect to find in a group of 20,000?

**2.** Choose a solution for **x ≥ 7**.

○ −1     ○ 5     ○ 6     ○ 7

**3.** Choose the trapezoid.

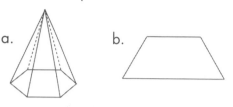

a.       b.

**4.** Find the product or quotient.

**a.** − 4 x (− 7)

**b.** 182 ÷ (− 2)

**5.** Cross out the unnecessary information. Then solve the problem.

Pedro had a very busy Saturday. After a 6:00 a.m. tennis match, he had breakfast with his grandmother, stopped at the corner store to get an ice cream cone, hurried to his Spanish lesson, stopped by the swimming pool for a quick dip, and then ate lunch with his buddies. At 2:00 p.m. he went to an early matinee and finally stopped at the soccer match to cheer for the team. Just on time he met his family for pizza. When he arrived home he fell into bed and slept 14 hours. His clock showed 10:00 a.m. when he opened his eyes the next morning. What time did Pedro fall into his bed?

**1.** Solve the equation.

$$x + 6\frac{3}{4} = 9\frac{1}{6}$$

**2.** The weather forecaster reported that it rained for three and one-half hours during the night. If the total rainfall was 2.25″, what was the average rainfall per hour?

**3.** Find the elapsed time between 6:33 a.m. and 7:20 p.m.

**4.** Mickey's hand moves around the clock face every minute. How far does the hand move in . . .

     a. 15 seconds?

     b. six minutes?

     c. seven hours?

*Have you considered hourglass time?*

**5.** Military time uses a 24-hour clock. The day begins at midnight, or 0000 hours. Complete the table to compare civilian time and military time.

| Civilian Time | Military Time | Civilian Time | Military Time |
|---|---|---|---|
| 12:00 a.m. | 0000 hours | 12:00 p.m. | _____ |
| 1:00 a.m. | 0100 hours | 1:00 p.m. | _____ |
| 2:00 a.m. | 0200 hours | 2:00 p.m. | _____ |
| 3:00 a.m. | 0300 hours | 3:00 p.m. | _____ |
| 4:00 a.m. | 0400 hours | 4:00 p.m. | _____ |
| 5:00 a.m. | _____ | 5:00 p.m. | _____ |
| 6:00 a.m. | _____ | 6:00 p.m. | _____ |
| 7:00 a.m. | _____ | 7:00 p.m. | _____ |
| 8:00 a.m. | _____ | 8:00 p.m. | _____ |
| 9:00 a.m. | _____ | 9:00 p.m. | _____ |
| 10:00 a.m. | _____ | 10:00 p.m. | _____ |
| 11:00 a.m. | _____ | 11:00 p.m. | _____ |

Would you rather use civilian or military time? Give reasons for your choice.

*Name*

The Clock Tower of the Palace of Westminster in London is about 316 feet tall. The tower has four sides, each with a large clock. Each clock face is a circle about 22 feet in diameter. The minute hands are about 12 feet long, measuring from the center of the clock face to the tip of the hand.

1. Write an expression that represents the circumference of the circle made by the tip of the minute hand in one hour.

2. What is the area of one of the clock faces?

3. Draw the clock tower. What is the surface area of the tower?

4. If the tower were 50 percent taller, how many times greater would the surface area be?

The Clock Tower of the Palace of Westminster

## 5. Challenge Problem

If the minute hand were twice as long, how much farther would it travel every hour? Explain the strategy you used to get your answer.

1. An ant brain has about $25 \times 10^4$ brain cells. A human brain has $10^{10}$ brain cells. Write a ratio to show a comparison between the numbers of cells in the two brains.

2. Find the value of the expression.

   **144 + 56 ÷ 4**

3. How many legs does a colony of 40,000 ants have? Write the number in standard notation and scientific notation.

4. True or false?

   **All squares are rectangles.**

Remember, ants are insects.

5. **Ants are super weightlifters. Bull ants weigh about 1 mg and can carry objects up to 50 times their weight. They haul their loads long distances and even climb trees with them!**

   **If humans could match this amazing strength, a 100-pound person would be able to pick up a small car, carry it seven or eight miles on his back, and then climb up a mountain peak still carrying the car!**

   **Imagine that humans were proportionally equal to the bull ant in their ability to carry and lift heavy objects. Write a proportion to determine what a 160-pound man could carry.**

1. Peter's mother despises ants. She buys a package of ant traps at $2.99 per pack every week. How much will she spend on ant traps in one year?

2. Solve for **a**.

   **a ÷ 0.05 = 140**

3. Write each fraction or mixed number as a decimal.

   a. $\frac{2}{5}$ _____

   b. $7\frac{5}{12}$ _____

   c. $\frac{42}{8}$ _____

4. Complete the statement.

   **64 cups equal _____ pints.**

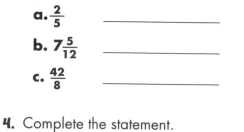

I guess I can forget about going to college.

OCT

5. Scientists studying an ant colony collected data that showed the range of the worker ant's life was 45–60 days. If an ant lived 53 days, is it accurate to say that the ant lived longer than the average ant? Explain your answer.

1. Write the next three terms and the rule for the number pattern.

   **81, 72, 63, _____, _____, _____**

2. Compare using **<** or **>**.

   a.  5 ___ –17     b.  –4 ___ – 13

   c. –19 ___ 7      d.  0 ___ –2

3. If one out of every 50 scouts from the anthill discovers a tasty treasure, how many treasures will be discovered by the 10,000-ant scouting unit?

4. Sal solved the problems. Check his work. Correct any mistakes.

   **a. –68 ÷ 4 = 17**

   **b. 154 ÷ (–11) = –14**

   **c. –5 x –41 = 200**

   **d. 1 x (–15) = 14**

5. Give the coordinates of the ants on the picnic cloth.

   a. _____, _____

   b. _____, _____

   c. _____, _____

   d. _____, _____

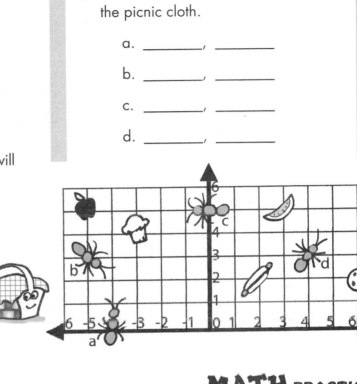

1. If one ant weighs one milligram, about how many ants would weigh one gram?

2. Find the surface area of a rectangular prism with the dimensions:

   **l = 14 m, w = 10 m, h = 8 m**

3. Express each mixed number in its lowest terms.

   a.  $\frac{16}{3}$

   b.  $\frac{49}{6}$

   c.  $\frac{67}{9}$

   d.  $\frac{103}{23}$

4. What part of the ant is shaded?

5. Explain the steps you would use to write 0.425 as a fraction in simplest form.

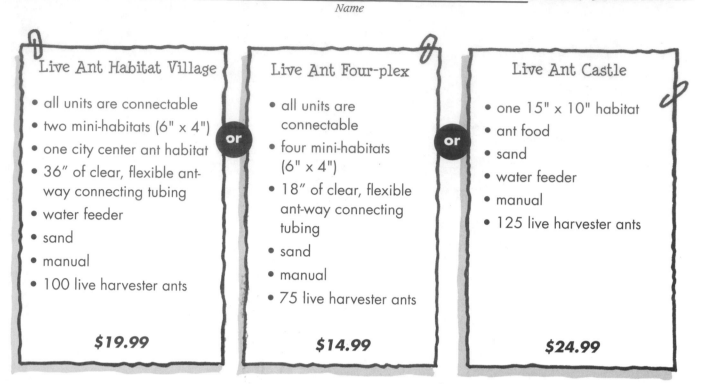

**Live Ant Habitat Village**

- all units are connectable
- two mini-habitats (6" x 4")
- one city center ant habitat
- 36" of clear, flexible ant-way connecting tubing
- water feeder
- sand
- manual
- 100 live harvester ants

**$19.99**

or

**Live Ant Four-plex**

- all units are connectable
- four mini-habitats (6" x 4")
- 18" of clear, flexible ant-way connecting tubing
- sand
- manual
- 75 live harvester ants

**$14.99**

or

**Live Ant Castle**

- one 15" x 10" habitat
- ant food
- sand
- water feeder
- manual
- 125 live harvester ants

**$24.99**

Charles wants to buy an ant farm for his little sister.

1. Compare the cost of the three ant farms.

   a. What is the difference in cost between the Village and the Castle?

   b. What is the difference between the Castle and the Four-plex?

   c. What is the difference between the Village and the Four-plex?

2. Considering only the cost of the ants, what is the cost per ant for the Four-plex?

3. Compare the viewing area of the Four-plex vs. the Castle. Remember ants may be viewed from any side of the structure. Which set has the greater viewing area?

4. If the tax is six percent and Charles has $40.00, will he be able to purchase a Village and a Four-plex?

# 5. Challenge Problem

In your opinion, which set is the best value? Explain your reasoning.

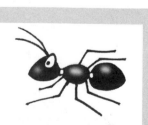

**1.** The estimated population of New Zealand is 4,035,461. What is the value of the digit 3 in the number?

**2.** About 21 percent of the population is under the age of 14. About how many New Zealanders are under 14? (Round to the nearest whole number.)

**3.** Solve the problem. Round to the nearest hundredth. **62 |1,881**

**4.** Find the next two terms in the pattern:

  **4, 6, 9, 13, 18, . . .**

*Did you know there are no mammals native to New Zealand?*

**5.** Chooose the rectangles that are similar to rectangle ABCD? Explain how you can tell.

  a. rectangle with sides of 7" and 3"

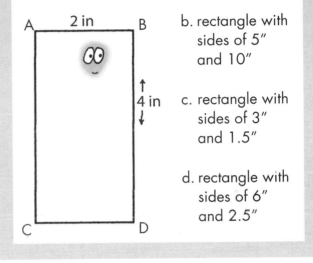

  b. rectangle with sides of 5" and 10"

  c. rectangle with sides of 3" and 1.5"

  d. rectangle with sides of 6" and 2.5"

**1.** Write each number in expanded form using powers of ten.

  a. **8,742**    b. **81,573**    c. **9,402,004**

**2.** Solve the equation.

  **x ÷ 5 = 3.5**

**3.** Wendy wants to see some whales off the coast of Kaikoura. She can take a half-hour flight for $65.00 or an hour-long boat excursion for $115.00. Use mental math to determine which method of watching whales is less expensive per minute.

*Watching whales can get expensive.*

**4.** Check the division.

$$\begin{array}{r} .8 \\ 4.2\overline{)33.6} \\ \underline{336} \end{array}$$

**5.** Five U.S. dollars are worth about seven and a half New Zealand dollars. Set up proportions and determine the New Zealand dollar equivalents.

  **a. $8.00 US =**

  **b. $1.00 US =**

  **c. $20.00 US =**

**1.** Helen went from the summit of Aoraki–Mount Cook, New Zealand's highest point at 3,754 m, to the edge of the Pacific Ocean, New Zealand's lowest point at 0 m. Express her change in elevation as an integer.

**2.** Which angle is not congruent with angle ABC?

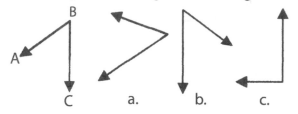

**3.** The forecast calls for a two-thirds chance of rain for each of the next three days. What is the probability that it will rain on two of the three days? Show the strategy you used to solve the problem.

**4.** Solve the problem.    $-112 \div (-14) =$ _____

**5.** What is the difference between the temperature on January 4 and the temperature on July 4?

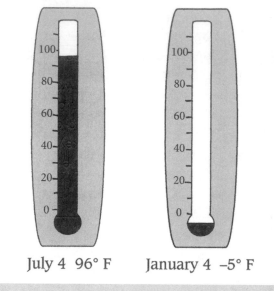

July 4  96° F        January 4  −5° F

**1.** Use the table. Determine the average size of blue whales and the average size of humpback whales. What is the difference between the two averages?

**Whale Watching in the Waters off New Zealand**

| Blue Whale estimated weight | Humpback Whale estimated weight |
|---|---|
| #1—11/7—125,000 kg | #1—11/7—48,000 kg |
| #2—11/7—136,000 kg | #2—11/8—29,000 kg |
| #3—11/8—132,000 kg | #3—11/8—34,000 kg |
| #4—11/9—129,000 kg | #4—11/8—27,000 kg |

**2.** Write each fraction as a percent.

　　a. $\frac{7}{8}$　　　　b. $\frac{1}{4}$　　　　c. $\frac{44}{55}$

**3.** Change the fraction $\frac{39}{12}$ to an improper fraction and then reduce it to its simplest form.

**4.** Solve the problem.    $12\frac{1}{4} \times 6\frac{2}{7}$

**5.** When you convert metric measurements (for example, when you change meters to centimeters or milligrams to grams), how do you decide whether to multiply or divide? State your answer as a rule.

I'm so confused.

## New Zealand Friday

*The Lord of the Rings* trilogy was filmed in New Zealand. New Zealand-born filmmaker Peter Jackson filmed the three films in various locations around the islands. The rolling hills of Matamata became Hobbiton, while the volcanic region of Mt. Ruapehu transformed into the fiery Mt. Doom where Sauron forged The Ring; and Queenstown, New Zealand's adventure capital, was the setting for numerous scenes, including the Eregion Hills and the Pillars of Argonath.

Over 2,000 people were employed during production; prop builders, set creators, make-up artists, and costume designers worked like elves to create Middle Earth. New Zealanders made thousands of props, including armor, weaponry, and 1,600 pairs of prosthetic feet and ears. *The Lord of the Rings* trilogy was filmed over 274 days, using 350 sets in more than 150 locations all over New Zealand. Filming in National Parks meant plants were uprooted to make room for the sets, temporarily housed in big custom-made nurseries, then replanted at the end of the shoot. In Queenstown, the site of heavy battle scenes, up to 1,100 people were on set each day. To protect plants from foot traffic, a massive amount of red carpet was laid. Location people also had to make sure they didn't destroy cultural symbols.

*The Lord of the Rings*
*trilogy, by J.R.R. Tolkien,*
*sells tens of thousands*
*of copies every year.*

1. What statistics do you need to determine the average number of people on the set during the two-week shooting of battle scenes in Queenstown? Is that information included in this article?

2. In addition to the live sets, the filmmakers used 64 miniature sets. The miniature sets were $\frac{1}{12}$ scale. If the Black Gate was 45' tall in the miniature set, how tall would it have been in real life? Set up a proportion to solve the problem.

3. The commissary served breakfast for the crew and actors on the set for the Siege of Minas Tirith. They used 1,440 eggs and 400 loaves of bread. If the cooks allowed two and a half eggs per person, how many did they expect to feed?

4. Before *The Return of the King* was released, records showed that the first film in the trilogy, *Fellowship of the Ring*, had earned $313.4 M in North America and $546.9 M internationally. Write both numbers in standard notation. Then determine what percentage of the total earnings are represented by the earnings in North America.

*Every reel*
*is a real masterpiece.*

## 5. Challenge Problem

Filming the trilogy is estimated to have cost about $270 M. What was the average filming cost per day?

**1.** Check the problem. Correct any errors.

$$
\begin{array}{r}
278 \\
\times\ 69 \\
\hline
2502 \\
\underline{1676\ \ } \\
19262
\end{array}
$$

**2.** Name the figure.

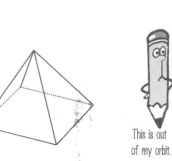

**3.** Simplify the expression.

$$92 + 42$$

**4.** Each container of water that the shuttle takes to the space station weighs 90 pounds. If the astronauts want to limit the water portion of cargo to 10.8 x 10² pounds, how many containers can they take?

This is out
of my orbit.

**5.** It takes the International Space Station 91.61 minutes to orbit the earth. Round the number to the nearest minute and estimate how many orbits the station can make in one day. About how many orbits per year?

Make a table to show the orbits completed from 1998 until today.

**1.** The Space Station is about 380 kilometers up in space. How many miles is that? Think of a place you know that is about that same distance from where you live.

**2.** Solve for n.

$$n \div 1.2 = 9$$

**3.** Write the number in expanded form using powers of 10.

**6,472,104**

**4.** Find the percentage.

**90% of 270 =**

I'll probably
swing by sometime.

**5.** Complete the puzzle. Use each digit –1 to 9 once and only once. Each of the two points and their connecting mid-point must equal nine.

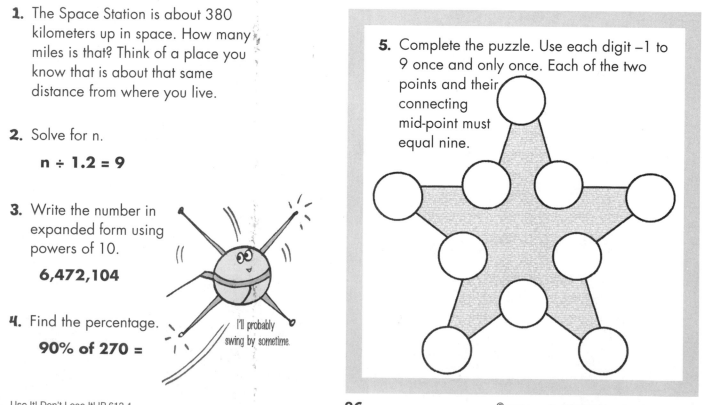

# WEDNESDAY WEEK 28 _____ MATH PRACTICE

*Name*

**1.** Find a if a, b, and c represent the length of the sides of a right triangle and c is the hypoteneuse.

**a = _____ , b = 9, c = 15**

**2.** What two things do you need to know to determine the surface area of the solar panels? Do you have enough information to find the area?

**The International Space Station is not just the biggest thing humans have put in space; it is also one of the brightest objects shining in the sky when the sun reflects off its four 240-foot-long solar panels.**

**3.** The forecast calls for a 50 percent chance of strong wind and rain for the next five days. What is the probability that the shuttle will have a sunny day for take-off tomorrow?

**4.** Find the square root. $\sqrt{484}$

I'm not really a square.

**5.** Name the point with the given coordinates.
a. (3, 1)     c. (−2, −3)
b. (−5, 3)    d. (2, −4)

# THURSDAY WEEK 28 _____ MATH PRACTICE

*Name*

**1.** The Space Shuttle travels at about five miles per second. A bullet exits a gun at about 2,500 feet per second. Explain the steps you must go through to compare the two speeds. Which is faster?

**2.** Do the two ratios form a **proportion**? Justify your answer.

$\frac{64}{128}$          $\frac{5}{10}$

**3.** Solve the problem.  $\frac{4}{11} \div 8 =$

**4.** Write an **inequality** for the graph.

**5.** The class is making a giant diagram of the space station. It will be 75 inches long and 50 inches wide. They will draw the diagram on a grid of $6\frac{1}{4}$" squares. How many squares will there be in the grid?

Need some help?

Use It! Don't Lose It! IP 613-1

Building the ISS required more than 50 flights. The table reports information about eight of the initial assembly flights.

| Element | Launch Vehicle | Launch Date | Length | Diameter | Mass |
|---------|---------------|-------------|--------|----------|------|
| Zarya FGB | Proton Rocket | 11/20/98 | 12.6 m | 4.1 m | 19,323 kg |
| Unity Node 1 | Endeavour | 12/4/98 | 5.49 m | 4.57 m | 11,612 kg |
| Service Module | Proton Rocket | 7/12/00 | 13.1.m | 4.15 m | 19,050 kg |
| Z1 Truss | Discovery | 10/11/00 | 4.9 m | 4.2 m | 8,755 kg |
| Solar Array | Endeavour | 11/30/00 | 73.2 m | 10.7 m | 15,900 kg |
| Destiny | Atlantis | 2/7/01 | 8.53 m | 4.27 m | 14,515 kg |
| Canadarm 2 | Endeavour | 4/19/01 | 17.6 m | 0.354 m | 4,899 kg |
| Joint Airlock | Atlantis | 7/12/01 | 5.5 m | 4 m | 6,064 kg |

For each question, note the statistics that you need to solve the problem. Then solve it.

**1.** What is the largest element transported to ISS in terms of size?

**2.** What is the largest element transported to ISS in terms of weight?

Did the answer to this question surprise you?

What factors might have caused the discrepancy?

**3.** What percentage of the first eight assembly flights were flown by the Space Shuttle Atlantis?

**4.** How many days are represented by the first ten expeditions?

## NUMBER OF DAYS ON MISSION

| Expedition | Duration | Expedition | Duration |
|-----------|----------|-----------|----------|
| 1 | 141 | 6 | 161 |
| 2 | 167 | 7 | 185 |
| 3 | 129 | 8 | 195 |
| 4 | 196 | 9 | 186 |
| 5 | 185 | 10 | 193 |

# 5. Challenge Problem

What is the range of the data?
What is the mean of the data?
Give your answer to the nearest day.

1. The workers in the zoo nursery get to name the baby animals by drawing names from a hat. On Tuesday six nursery workers each write a name for the baby hippo on a slip of paper and put it into the hat. Two of the workers suggest Tubs. What is the probability that the name picked will be Tubs?

2. Find the volume of the snow cone cup. (Round to the nearest half-inch.)

$V = \frac{1}{3}Bh$

$B$ = area of base

3 in

4 in

3. Find the missing number.

**28,000 ÷ ☐ = 40**

4. Solve.    $\frac{1}{7}x = 800 - x$

5. Mark the information that is needed to answer the question.

**How many spectators stopped by to see the baby hippo?**

○ 625 visited before noon.

○ Many of the early visitors went home around 1:00 p.m.

○ Mother hippo ate at 2:00 p.m.

○ The afternoon crowd was twice the size of the morning crowd.

What are you staring at?

1. Leroy has a job as a guide at the zoo, but he spends a lot of time watching the monkeys. In fact, he watches them about 3.8 hours a day, five days a week. Over a 12-week summer, about how much time does Leroy spend monkey watching?

2. Write the missing numbers in the pattern.

**9812, 8723, _____, 6545,**

**_____, 4367, 3278**

3. The scout troop receives a group discount of 25 percent on the price of admission. What will it cost for 12 scouts and two leaders to visit the zoo?

Adults $4.00
Students $2.50

4. The monkey eats a banana and a few nuts. Which is the best estimate for the amount of food the monkey has eaten?

    a. two gallons of fruit      c. one quart of fruit

    b. one half pint of fruit     d. one ounce of fruit

5. Rick has a dollar bill and he needs change so he can buy some food to feed the pygmy goats. There are 293 ways to make change for a dollar. Name ten different ways here.

1. _____
2. _____
3. _____
4. _____
5. _____
6. _____
7. _____
8. _____
9. _____
10. _____

1. The San Diego Zoo had 3,085,038 visitors, and the San Diego Wild Animal Park had 1,402,906 visitors. Is it accurate to say that the zoo had about three times as many visitors as the wild animal park? Give a reason for your answer.

2. The answer to the problem is 0. What is the problem?

   a. $-20 \times -30 - (600)$

   b. $(-300 + 100) \div 4$

   c. $100 \div -4 + 50 + 75$

3. Name one pair of corresponding angles.

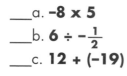

4. Order the expressions from greatest to least.

   ___ a. **-8 x 5**

   ___ b. **$6 \div -\frac{1}{2}$**

   ___ c. **12 + (-19)**

5. What is the correct order for performing the operations to solve this problem?

   **The trainer has taught the bear to walk across a narrow 24' platform.**

   **The bear stood up on its back legs and walked one-third of the distance.**

   **Then it gave a grunt and plopped off the platform onto the ground.**

   **How far did the bear walk on the platform?**

*Don't try this after lunch.*

1. Write the answer in lowest terms.

   $$\frac{7}{9} \times \frac{5}{7} = \underline{\hspace{1cm}}$$

2. The first dolphin show lasted two-thirds of an hour. The second show lasted 45 minutes. The trainer said that the second show was one-four hour longer than the first. Is she right?

3. $7\frac{2}{3} + 4\frac{5}{12} =$

4. Peanuts, the baby Asian elephant, weighed 360 pounds when she was born. She will weigh about 11,000 pounds as an adult. Express her adult weight as a percentage of her newborn weight.

*Mom called me Peanut, too.*

5.

Write a fraction to show:

   a. the number of occupied cages

   b. the number of animals without tails

   c. the number of four-footed animals

   d. the number of animals with fur

## Heavy Facts

### African Elephant

ear . . . . . . . . . . . 110 pounds

trunk . . . . . . . . 400 pounds

tusk . . . . . 440 pounds/pair

tail . . . . . . . . . . . 22 pounds

## Fast Facts

falcon . . . . . . 150 mph

cheetah. . . . . . 70 mph

antelope . . . . . 60 mph

lion . . . . . . . . . 50 mph

coyote. . . . . . . 43 mph

hyena . . . . . . . 40 mph

dragonfly . . . . 36 mph

giraffe. . . . . . . 32 mph

elephant . . . . . 25 mph

snail . . . . . . . 0.03 mph

1. Can you make a reasonable assumption that an elephant weighs only a little more than 1,000 pounds? Explain your reasoning.

2. How many hours would it take a snail to go one mile?

3. How much faster is an antelope than a giraffe?

4. Compare the elephant's speed with the falcon's speed.

## 5. Challenge Problem

Make a graph to show a plausible number of babies produced by different zoo animals.

Follow this procedure.

1. Find the midpoint of the range of babies for the animal.

2. Round to the nearest whole number.

3. Graph the number of offspring.

prairie dog . . . . . . . . . . . . . 2–10 pups
wolf . . . . . . . . . . . . . . . . . . . . 4–7 pups
tiger . . . . . . . . . . . . . . . . . . 2–3 cubs
leopard . . . . . . . . . . . . . . . 1–6 kittens
lion . . . . . . . . . . . . . . . . . . 3–4 cubs
kangaroo . . . . . . . . . . . . . . one joey
hedgehog. . . . . . . . . . . . . . 1–7 babies
rhinoceros . . . . . . . . . . . . . one calf

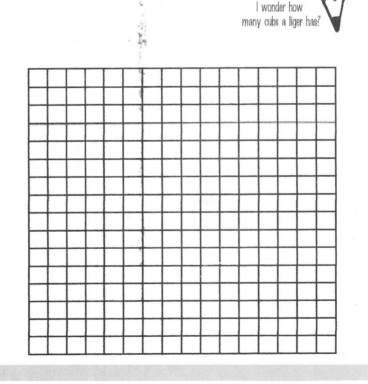

Have you ever heard of a liger? It's a cross between a lion and a tiger.

Animal Trivia

I wonder how many cubs a liger has?

1. In the United States about 120 billion elevator rides are taken every year. About how many elevator rides per day does the figure represent? (Assume a non-leap year.)

2. What is the **prime factorization** of 120?

3. Find the surface area of the rectangular prism with the given dimensions.

   **l = 5 cm, w = 3 cm, h = 6 cm**

4. Evaluate the expression for x = 9.

   **42 (x – 5)**

I make corrections using my head.

5. John is stuck in the elevator and is waiting for help. He decides to play a game using the button pad. He will start by pushing one button in the bottom row. He will push one button in each row. He must move only one space up or one space diagonally up in each turn. If he presses 1 first, will he be able to add all six pushes and score above a total of 83? Give an example that proves your answer.

1. The first passenger elevator was used in a five-story department store in New York on March 23, 1857. How long ago was that?

2. Underline the information that you need to know to solve the problem. Name any additional information that you need.

   **Elevators in Sam's building travel about 1,000 feet per second. Sam gets on the elevator at the first floor, travels up to the sixth floor, down to the third floor, and back to the first floor. How long did he spend on the elevator?**

3. Write the decimal in words.

   **0.503**

4. Solve the problem. **209.4 ÷ 8 =**

5. The elevator in the Petronas Towers in Kuala Lumpur moves 232 people from the 24th floor to the 37th floor every five minutes. If the actual elevator travel time is 28.6 seconds, how much time is taken loading and unloading passengers? How much time in every hour is actual elevator travel time?

   Set up a proportion to determine the answer.

How many people did you take up today?
More than you!

1. Brianna gets on the elevator on the forty-second floor. She gets off on the twenty-seventh floor. Express her elevator ride as an integer.

2. Two-year-old Brett loves to ride in the elevator. He boards on the third floor. The elevator goes up ten floors, down four floors, up six floors, down seven floors, and finally after the elevator goes up one floor, he gets off. What floor is he on? How many floors did he pass by or visit?

3. The hotel has three elevators on the right side and two elevators on the left side. What is the probability that JoEllen will get on an elevator on the right side?

4. Imagine the patterns folded into figures. Name the figures.

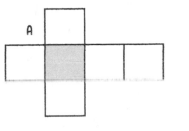

5. Complete the function table for the following rule:

**Output = Input ÷ – 2**

| Input | Output |
|-------|--------|
| −10   | _____ |
| 0     | _____ |
| 12    | _____ |

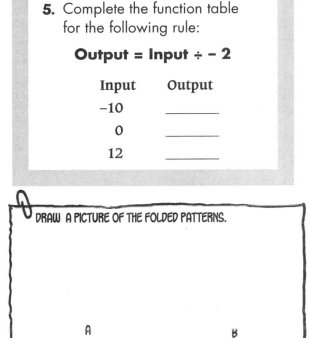

DRAW A PICTURE OF THE FOLDED PATTERNS.

A          B

1. Write each decimal as a fraction or mixed number in its simplest form.
   a. 4.20
   b. 91.18

2. The world's fastest passenger elevator, located in Taipei, runs at a top speed of 1,000 meters per minute when ascending, and 600 meters per minute on the way down. How much faster is the ascending speed than the descending speed?

3. Solve the problem.     $x - \frac{1}{10} = \frac{1}{2}$

4. Mandy pays $3.25 for a ticket to the observation deck on the 25th floor. How much does the elevator ride cost per floor?

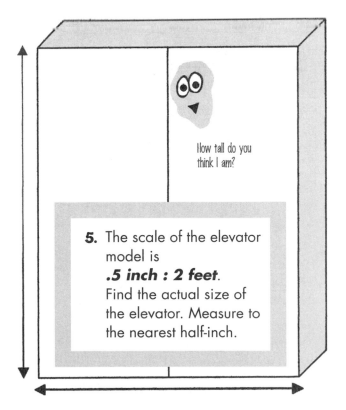

How tall do you think I am?

5. The scale of the elevator model is **.5 inch : 2 feet**. Find the actual size of the elevator. Measure to the nearest half-inch.

Find each of the following:

**1.** the area of the floor of the elevator

**2.** the volume of the elevator

**3.** the perimeter of the door opening

**4.** area of the circular design (to the nearest inch)

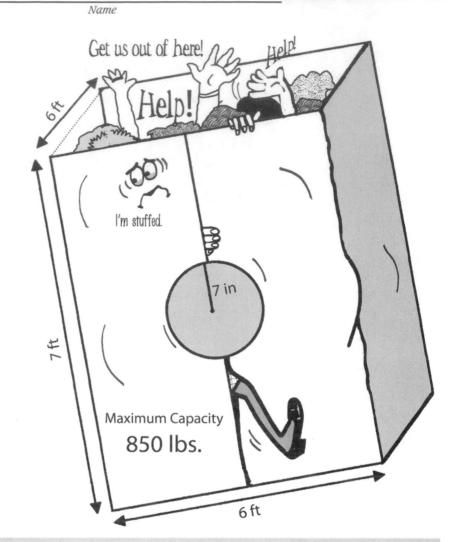

Get us out of here!    Help!

Help!

6 ft

I'm stuffed.

7 in

7 ft

Maximum Capacity
850 lbs.

6 ft

## 5. Challenge Problem

The first four passengers to get on the elevator weigh 85 pounds, 120 pounds, 230 pounds, and 185 pounds. Four passengers are waiting to get on when the elevator stops on the next floor. Passenger A weighs 185 pounds, Passenger B weighs 60 pounds, Passenger C weighs 175 pounds, and Passenger D weighs 50 pounds.

Determine two different sets of passengers that can board the elevator safely.

　1.

　2.

**1.** In 1990 the Cat Fancier's Association registered 84,729 cats in the United States. In 2000 they registered 49,551. Compare the two numbers and make a statement about the registrations.

**2.** What percent of 1990's registrations do the 2000 registrations represent?

**3.** Which angle is about 150°?

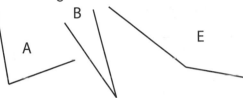

**4.** Solve the problem.

**915 x 27 =**

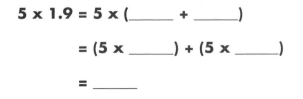

**5.** Write an inequality to compare the number of Maine Coon cats to the number of Siamese and Exotic cats.

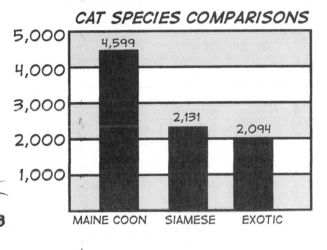

CAT SPECIES COMPARISONS

MAINE COON 4,599
SIAMESE 2,131
EXOTIC 2,094

**1.** There are 70,000,000 cats in the United States. Write that number as a multiple of ten.

**2.** Order the decimals from the least to the greatest.

**8.34    83.4    .834    834    .0834    8,340**

___  ___  ___  ___  ___  ___

**3.** Solve the problem.    **0.715 x 0.07 =**

**4.** Use the **Distributive Property** to simplify the expression.

**5 x 1.9 = 5 x (_____ + _____)**

**= (5 x _____) + (5 x _____)**

**= _____**

**5.** A Happy Cat Starter Kit is on sale for $37.58. Hazel picked out a domed litter box for $19.99, a scoop for $1.02, a litter mat for $10.80, and a 7-lb bag of litter for $6.99. Is the starter kit a better value? Justify your answer.

1. Write three numbers that are between −2 and −5. Are all of these numbers integers? Explain.

2. The litter has white, black, and tiger-striped kittens. If you choose one at random, **P(black)** $= \frac{1}{4}$. If there are two black kittens, how many kittens are there in all?

3. The average number of cats in a cat-owning household is 2.1. There are 2,280 cat-owning households in Golden, CO. About how many cats live in Golden? (Round to the nearest whole number.)

4. Round the number to the nearest tenth.

    **8,074.68**

5. The kittens' playpen is a huge circular basket with a radius of 2.5 ft. What is the area of the playpen?

At last, room to roll around.

1. The American Veterinary Association has developed a formula for determining the number of cat-owning households in a community.

    **0.316 x total number of households = number of cat-owning households**

    There are 2,185,992 households in Tennessee. How many are cat-owning households?

2. Express each fraction in its lowest form.

    **a.** $\frac{28}{42}$    **b.** $\frac{42}{70}$    **c.** $\frac{8}{32}$

3. $12\frac{1}{4} \times 3\frac{1}{2} =$

4. Give the next three numbers in the pattern.

    **5 ,        $4\frac{3}{4}$ ,        $4\frac{1}{2}$ ,**

    _____  _____  _____

5. Use the scale to determine the length of the kittens' tails.

    *0.5 cm = 2"*

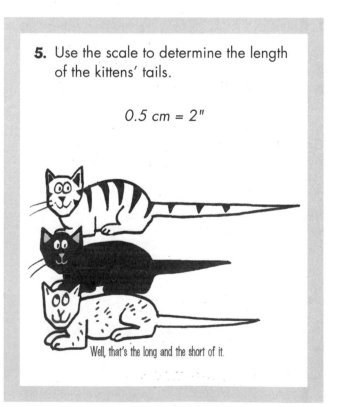

Well, that's the long and the short of it.

**1.** Complete the table.

| Cats | Paws | Ears | Whiskers | Tails |
|------|------|------|----------|-------|
| 1    | 4    | 2    | 12       | 1     |
| 5    |      |      |          |       |
| 10   |      |      |          |       |
| 20   |      |      |          |       |
| 50   |      |      |          |       |

**2.** Write a formula for determining the number of paws (p) on a given number of cats (c).

**3.** Write a formula for determining the number of tails (t) on a given number of cats (c).

**4.** a. Use your formula to find the number of paws for 3,452 cats.

b. Use your formula to find the number of paws for all 70 million cats in the U.S.

## 5. Challenge Problem

Use your formula to find the number of tails for seven dozen cats.

1. The score for the word is 16 points. What's the word?

2. True or false? **An obtuse triangle can have three sides of equal length.**

3. Solve the problem. **67,302 x 503 =**

4. Steve and Scott are playing in a Scrabble match. The winner is the player to receive the highest average game score. Use the data below to determine the winner.

|  | Game 1 | Game 2 | Game 3 | Game 4 |
|---|---|---|---|---|
| **Steve** | 218 | 296 | 278 | 301 |
| **Scott** | 254 | 264 | 276 | 287 |

5. Transfer the data in problem four to a line graph.

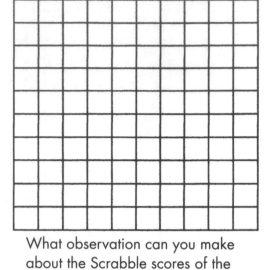

What observation can you make about the Scrabble scores of the two players?

1. The first Scrabble game took an hour and thirty minutes. The second game was over in only 55 minutes. What is the difference in time between the two matches?

That's a timely question.

2. Solve the problem. **22.984 ÷ .4 =**

3. Tell which consecutive whole numbers the square root is between.

$$\sqrt{29}$$

4. A number N has both 4 and 9 as factors. Name two additional factors other than one for the number N.

5. The Collector's Edition Scrabble game is on sale for 30 percent off the regular price of $29.95. Jill has a coupon for an additional ten percent off. What will she pay for the game?

**1.** At the end of the game, Elise has the following tiles left in her rack. The value of the tiles is subtracted from her score. Elise had 243 points as the round began. What was her final score?

**2.** Choose the statement that is not true.

- ○ $-9 < -7$
- ○ $-2 < 4$
- ○ $-6 > -5$
- ○ $-3 < 3$

**3.** A regulation Scrabble board has 15 squares down one side and 15 squares across the top. How many squares are on the board? There are eight triple word squares on the board. What percentage of the total squares are triple word squares?

**4.** Find the area of the parallelogram.

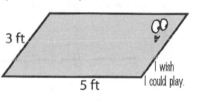

3 ft

5 ft

I wish I could play.

**5.** Estimate the number of vowels to the nearest whole number.

| Frequency of Vowels in Scrabble Words Played | | | | | |
|---|---|---|---|---|---|
| Letter | a | e | i | o | u |
| Frequency | 10% | 13% | 8% | 7% | 3% |

How many E tiles in 300 letters played?

How many U tiles in 183 letters played?

How many A tiles in 28 letters played?

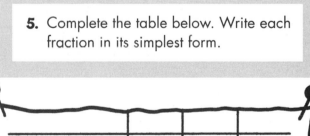

**1.** Roberto wants to create a giant scrabble game. He will make each letter tile two feet across. Determine the scale he should use to create the tiles if a normal-sized tile is a $\frac{3}{4}$" square.

**2.** Solve for **x**. $\frac{x}{8} = 20$

**3.** Solve the problem. $14\frac{1}{4} - 6\frac{3}{8} = $ _____

**4.** Belle's average think time before making a Scrabble play is 175 seconds. Rose's average think time is two and a half minutes. Which girl usually thinks longer before playing?

Timing is everything.

**5.** Complete the table below. Write each fraction in its simplest form.

| | | | |
|---|---|---|---|
| fraction | $\frac{13}{50}$ | | |
| decimal | | .96 | |
| percent | | | 42% |

Name

Q₁₀ R₁ E₁ E₁ M₃ D₂ D₂ I₁ F₄ S₁ E₁ T₁

There are 12 tiles remaining to be drawn.
Determine the probability of drawing
in order:

**1.** an **E** tile

**2.** a **Q** tile

**3.** a **D** tile

**4.** an **E** tile

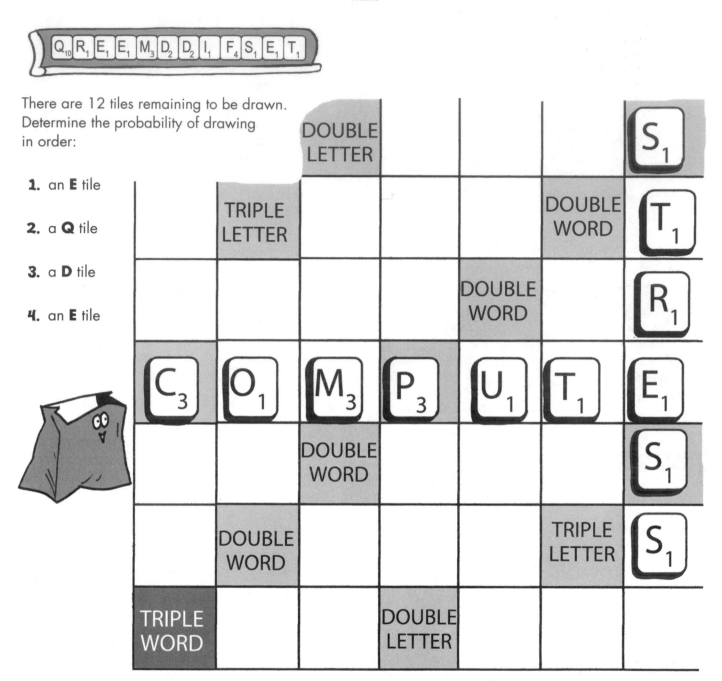

## 5. Challenge Problem

Form two different words using seven or less tiles in the letter bag and determine the score you would receive for each word if it were played across a double word score square.

1. A cluster of stars named M13 is a part of the constellation Hercules. There are $3 \times 10^5$ stars in the cluster. How many stars is that?

2. Find the least common multiple of seven and twelve.

3. Round each number to the nearest thousand.

   a. **2,875,890**

   b. **89,576**

   c. **520,721**

4. Our solar system is revolving around the center of the Galaxy at a speed of half a million miles per hour, but it still takes 200 million years for it to go around the Galaxy once. What conclusion can you draw about the size of the Galaxy?

5. Danny wants to buy a Zenith 60 x 600 telescope. He will also need an eyepiece, a moon filter, and a set of sky maps. He has saved $175.00. Estimate to determine whether he has enough money to order what he wants. Then do the actual math to check your estimate.

Look at that.

**This Week Only!**

*Big Savings* - 30% OFF

| ZENITH 60 X 600 TELESCOPE | $99.00 |
| EYEPIECE | $39.95 |
| SKY MAPS | $19.95 |
| MOON FILTER | $15.95 |

1. A small six-inch telescope helps you read the writing on a dime from 150 feet away. About how many meters is that?

2. What is the first step in solving the equation?

   $24(x + 4) = 32$

3. Identify the missing operation.

   $5.6 \_\_\_\_ 3,42 = 19.152$

4. Solve for h.

   $h \div 2.4 = 1.5$

Wow!
I didn't know numbers came that large.

5. Alpha Centauri is 4.35 light-years from the Sun. A light-year is the distance which light can travel in a year. Light is fast, so a light-year is a long way! The speed of light is about 299,792,458 meters per second.

   a. How many seconds are in a year?

   b. How many meters can light travel in a year?

Use It! Don't Lose It! IP 613-1

**1.** The astronomy club wants to visit the planetarium. The club has 16 student members and 20 adult members. Four of the adult members are over 65. Write an equation to show how to determine what they will pay to get in.

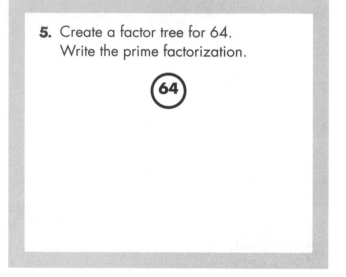

ADMISSION
ADULTS.................$4
STUDENTS...........$2
SENIORS.............$3

**2.** Solve the problems.

a. **–8 x 39 =**

b. **252 ÷ (–4) =**

c. **–27 x –6 =**

**3.** While the junior astronomers were stargazing, the temperature fell 16°. If the temperature when the evening started was 37°, what was the temperature when the astronomers adjourned for hot chocolate?

**4.** The weatherman predicted the probability of cloud-free stargazing was three chances in five. The astronomy club has one meeting each month. How many cloud-free nights will they probably have in one year?

**5.** Create a factor tree for 64. Write the prime factorization.

(64)

**1.** The most massive star known is R136a1, a star 155 times as massive as our Sun. The sun's mass is 1.989 x 1030 kg. How big is R136a1?

**2.** Choose the fraction that is not equivalent to $\frac{2}{3}$.

○ $\frac{12}{18}$   ○ $\frac{26}{39}$   ○ $\frac{28}{42}$   ○ $\frac{38}{54}$

**3.** $\frac{2}{3} \div \frac{1}{4} =$

**4.** Reduce the fractions to lowest terms.

a. $\frac{12}{50}$

b. $\frac{18}{90}$

c. $\frac{27}{42}$

d. $\frac{34}{51}$

**5.** Cory has completed this table. Check his computations to make sure that the chart is accurate. Correct any mistakes.

**Different Weights of the same object**

|  | scale | astronaut | piece of equipment |
|---|---|---|---|
| **Earth** | 1 pound | 86 pounds | 6,036 pounds |
| **Moon** | $\frac{1}{6}$ pound | 13 pounds | 1,006 pounds |
| **Venus** | $\frac{5}{6}$ pound | 173 pounds | 5,036 pounds |

I am *so* starstruck.

In most cases, the stars in constellations and asterisms are each very different distances from us. They only appear to be grouped because they lie in approximately the same direction. Look at the figure showing the stars of the Big Dipper. Their physical distance from the Earth is drawn to scale and shown by the dots on the lines. Numbers beside each star's name give that star's distance from Earth in light-years.

**1.** What is the average distance of the stars from the earth?

**2.** What is the range of distances?

**3.** Which star is the closest to Earth?

**4.** What is its relative distance compared to the star that is the most distant? Write this comparison as a ratio in the lowest terms.

EARTH

STARS– DISTANCE IN LIGHT YEARS

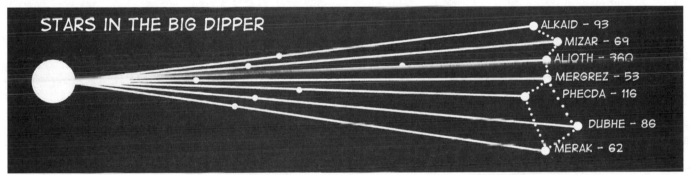

STARS IN THE BIG DIPPER

ALKAID – 93
MIZAR – 69
ALIOTH – 360
MERGREZ – 53
PHECDA – 116
DUBHE – 86
MERAK – 62

## 5. Challenge Problem

What kind of graph would best show the different distances?

Use It! Don't Lose It! IP 613-1

1. An individual porcupine has about 30,000 quills. That's $3 \times 10^4$ quills per porcupine. Use the number $3 \times 10^4$ and compute the number of quills on four porcupines.

2. What is the value of the **7** in **940,072,000**?

3. Choose the one that is not a quadrilateral.
   - ○ trapezoid
   - ○ parallelogram
   - ○ rhombus
   - ○ pentagon

4. Find the volume of the hedgehog's food dish.

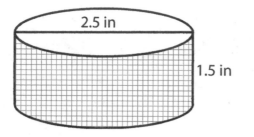

2.5 in

1.5 in

5. Name the pattern.

1. Franco wants to adopt a baby hedgehog, but his parents want to know what the hedgehog's food will cost per week. The hedgehog eats 1 oz of supplement mixed with 1 oz of kibble daily. Three times a week the hedgehog gets a Luv Bug treat (.25 oz). What is the cost of food per week?

   **Food Supplement** . . . . $10.00 for 2.5 lb bag

   **Kibble** . . . . . . . . . . . . . . $6.00 for 2.5 lb bag

   **Luv Bugs (dried crickets**
   **and wax worms)** . . . . . . . $2.00 for 3 oz

2. Find the product.

   **7.5(0.63)**

   Huh?

   LUV BUGS 3 oz./ $2.00

3. Find the quotient. **98.04 ÷ 2.4 =**

4. What is the GCF of **36** and **63**?

5. Complete the chart to show the three animals' relative weights.

| | Weight | Length | Pounds/Inch |
|---|---|---|---|
| Echidna | 10 pounds | 15" | _____ |
| Hedgehog | $1\frac{1}{4}$ pound | $6\frac{1}{2}$" | _____ |
| Porcupine | 30 pounds | $2\frac{1}{4}$ feet | _____ |

**1.** Solve the problems.

    **a. (– 8) + (–17) = ___**

    **b. 9 – (–9) = ___**

    **c. –4 + (–6) = ___**

**2.** Which two angles are supplementary?

**3.** What is the square root of 121?

**4.** A porcupine moves at the speed of 2.2 mph. The distance from its den to the lake is .4 miles. If the porcupine leaves home at noon, what time will it arrive at the lake?

**5.** The Porcupine Patrol is on the lookout for porcupines. Make a frequency table and a line plot for their set of data.

**Porcupines Spotted**
3, 1, 4, 2, 4, 1, 4, 2, 4, 2, 1

**1.** The ratio of the weight of a female echidna to a male echidna is about $\frac{2}{3}$. Set up a proportion and estimate the weight of a female if the male weighs 5 kg.

**2.** If **x** is a prime number greater than 2, does **x + 1** represent a prime or a composite number? Explain.

**3.** Cross out the information that is unnecessary; then solve the problem.

    **The average length of an echidna's snout is 7 cm. It is stiff enough to break up logs and termite mounds when the echidna is searching for food. One adult echidna measures 42 cm. What fraction of the echidna's length does its snout represent?**

**4.** Find the permutations of the letters in the word **BIG**.

**5.** What percent of each grid is shaded?

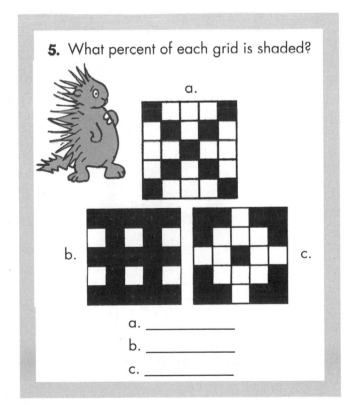

a. _____
b. _____
c. _____

_____
*Name*

Solve the problems to answer the riddle.

**a.** 4,282 + 7,518

**b.** 2,408 + 946

**c.** 5,417 + 2,039

**d.** 973 - 268

**e.** 427 - 193

**f.** 629 - 382

**g.** 956 x 36

**h.** 371 x 79

**i.** 75 x 104

| KEY | | |
|---|---|---|
| T = 705 | Y = 7,800 | F = 29,309 |
| A = 11,800 | B = 7,456 | E = 234 |
| O = 3,354 | H = 247 | L = 34,416 |

What do a porcupine and a bar of Ivory soap have in common?

Not much, by the look of it.

d. __ f. __ e. __ i. __ c. __ b. __ d. __ f. __ h. __ g. __ b. __ a. __ d.

### Simple Machines

**1.** Find the volume of the rectangular prism.

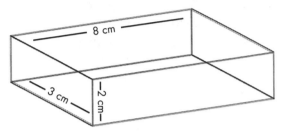

8 cm

3 cm

2 cm

**2.** 8,323,004 ÷ 20 =

**3.** Which two shapes are **congruent**?

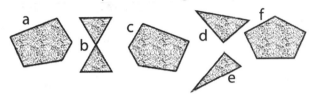

a  b  c  d  f  e

**4.** Round to the nearest thousand. **999,826**

**5.** Omar's dad will use a pulley to lift the heavy crates. He wants to make as few lifts as possible. The pulley can lift 4,500 pounds at a time. Organize the crates into groups. Make as few groups as possible.

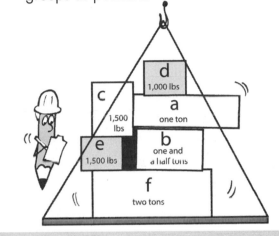

c — 1,500 lbs
d — 1,000 lbs
a — one ton
e — 1,500 lbs
b — one and a half tons
f — two tons

**1.** How many minutes are in five hours and 45 minutes?

**2.** Each shelf requires three supports. Write a formula you could use to determine the number of supports needed for any number of shelves.

**3.** Solve the problem. (Round to the nearest hundredth)

9,754.6 ÷ 4.02

**4.** Measure the nail to the nearest cm.

**5.** Many tools are combinations of simple machines. Choose a combination of tools that includes a wedge, lever, screw, and wheel and axle. The total cost of the tools must not exceed $10.00.

$8.99 A hand drill includes a wheel and axle, a wedge, and a screw.

$.59 A screw includes a screw.

$2.69 A hammer includes a lever and a wedge.

$2.19 A paint roller is a wheel and axle.

$1.49 A screwdriver is a wedge.

$.07 A nail is a wedge.

$6.50 A crow bar includes a lever and a wedge.

1. How would the volume of a cube change if its dimensions were doubled? Give an example to support your statement.

2. Adam has a bag of nails. There are twenty-one nails in the bag. Seven of the nails are 3" long and all the others are 2". What is the probability of randomly choosing a 3" nail? Express your answer in lowest terms.

3. Use mental math to solve the problem.

   **−4 x (−23) =**

   *He really hit the nail on the head.*

4. Draw a long narrow cylinder.

5. Measure force by dividing **a** the distance from the fulcrum to the load by **b** the distance from the fulcrum to the effort, and multiplying the answer by the weight of the load. The force is expressed in Newtons.

   **force = $\frac{a}{b}$ x weight of load**

   Determine the force needed to lift a load of 50 pounds with the Lifts-All Lever and the Effort-less Lever.

| | Lifts-All | Effort-less |
|---|---|---|
| **Distance from fulcrum to load** | 6 | 3 |
| **Distance from fulcrum to effort** | 14 | 9 |

1. Order the wrenches from the smallest to the largest.

   **Stand 15-piece Wrench Set (sizes in inches)**

   $\frac{1}{4}$,  $\frac{9}{16}$,  $\frac{7}{8}$,  $\frac{5}{16}$,  $\frac{5}{8}$,

   $\frac{15}{16}$,  $\frac{3}{8}$,  $\frac{11}{16}$,  1,  $\frac{7}{16}$,

   $\frac{3}{4}$,  $1\frac{1}{16}$,  $\frac{1}{3}$,  $\frac{13}{16}$,  $1\frac{1}{8}$

2. Stefan needs a $\frac{6}{16}$-inch wrench. Which wrench in the set should he use?

3. Drew chose a $\frac{7}{16}$-inch wrench. It is too big for the bolt. He tries a $\frac{5}{16}$-inch wrench, and it is too small. What size wrench will work?

4. Which wrench measures .625 inches?

5. How much bigger is the largest wrench in the set than the smallest?

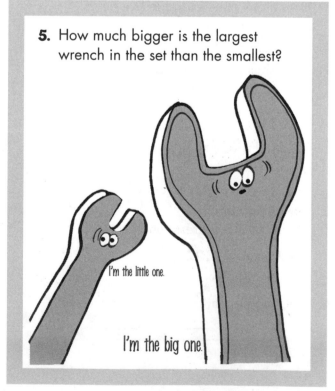

I'm the little one.

I'm the big one.

**1.**

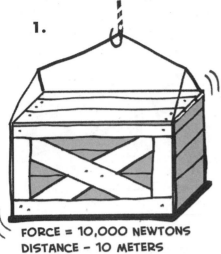

FORCE = 10,000 NEWTONS
DISTANCE - 10 METERS

**3.**

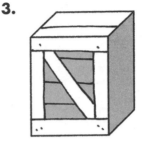

FORCE = 5,000 NEWTONS
DISTANCE = 150 METERS

**2.**

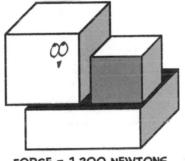

FORCE = 1,200 NEWTONS
DISTANCE = 575 METERS

Scientists have developed a formula for determining the amount of work done.

### Work = force x distance

So the amount of work that is done in moving a box of books from the floor to the shelf, for instance, is determined by the force it takes to move the books and the distance the books are moved. Force is expressed in units called Newtons.
Work is expressed in units called joules. A joule is equal to one Newton-meter.

**4.**

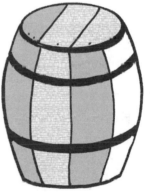

FORCE = 2,000 NEWTONS
DISTANCE = 20 METERS

## Challenge Problem

Determine the work done in each of the problems shown.

**5.**

FORCE = 25 NEWTONS
DISTANCE = 2.5 METERS

1. Exactly 785 kite fliers showed up for the festival, and 510 were under the age of 16. What percent of the total did these participants represent? (Round your answer to the nearest percent.)

2. Find the length of **c**.
Remember: $a^2 + b^2 = c^2$

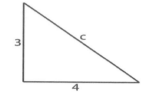

3. Solve the equation.

   **18k = 234**

4. Every student who participates in Kite Day is eligible to win a new kite. Suppose 100 students participate and there are 11 prize kites. The name of one student is drawn at random for each prize. Assuming you are eligible, what is the probability that you will win a kite?

**5.** Estimate in units the area of the kite.

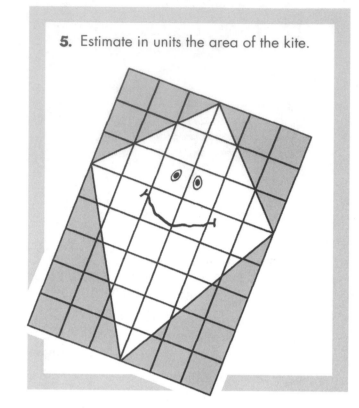

1. A shuttle leaves the parking lot every 20 minutes to take passengers to the kite festival. The first shuttle leaves at 7:00 a.m. What is the departure time closest to 1:55 p.m?

2. Write the decimal in words.

   **.086**

3. Check the problem for accuracy. Correct any mistakes.

$$\begin{array}{r} 63.26 \\ \times\ 3.05 \\ \hline 31630 \\ 189780 \\ \hline 22.1410 \end{array}$$

4. Write the next two terms and a rule for the number pattern.

   **7, 19, 31, 43, _____, _____**

**5.**

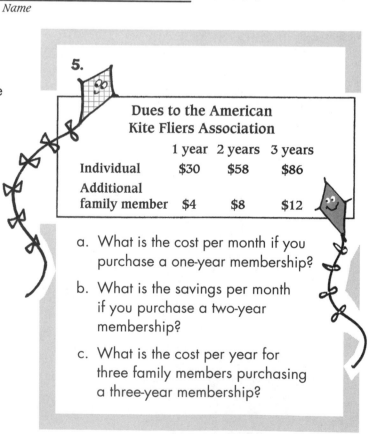

| Dues to the American Kite Fliers Association | | | |
|---|---|---|---|
| | 1 year | 2 years | 3 years |
| Individual | $30 | $58 | $86 |
| Additional family member | $4 | $8 | $12 |

a. What is the cost per month if you purchase a one-year membership?

b. What is the savings per month if you purchase a two-year membership?

c. What is the cost per year for three family members purchasing a three-year membership?

**1.** Write an inequality for the graph.

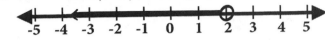

**2.** Draw a line of symmetry for the rectangle. Is there more than one possible correct answer?

**3.** Mac flew his kite with 30 feet of string unwound. Gradually he let out 27 more feet. He reeled 6 feet back until the kite stabilized, then he reeled in 10 more feet. How many feet are unwound?

**4.** Complete the function table if the rule is

**Output = Input ÷ (−2)**

| Input | Output |
|-------|--------|
| 18    |        |
| − 22  |        |
| 34    |        |

**5.** How many congruent triangles are in the kite? How many similar triangles?

**1.** In 1978 Kuzuhiko Asaba flew 4,128 kites on a single line. If the kites were six inches apart, how long was the line from the first kite to the last?

**2.** Write the fraction as a percent.

$$\frac{15}{25}$$

**3.** Kai sold half of his kite collection to Ana, half of the remaining kites to Fritz, and the last ten to Omar. How many kites did Kai sell?

**4.** Correct the following statement.

**Since 42 equals seven squared, and 21 equals seven times three, the GCF of 42 and 21 is seven.**

**5.** Make two simultaneous patterns on the kite tail. One must be an **ABBABB** pattern, and one must be an **ABCAABCA** pattern.

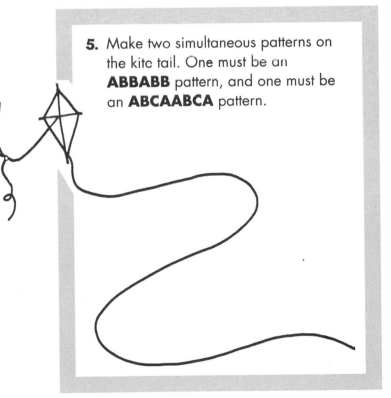

Use It! Don't Lose It! IP 613-1

## Challenge Problem

Jade wants to use double the size of the kite pattern. Use the diagram as a reference and draw a new kite pattern so that the kite is exactly two times larger than the original. Create a new list of materials.

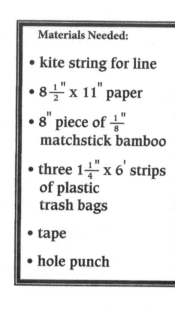

**Materials Needed:**

- kite string for line
- $8\frac{1}{2}"$ x $11"$ paper
- $8"$ piece of $\frac{1}{8}"$ matchstick bamboo
- three $1\frac{1}{4}"$ x $6'$ strips of plastic trash bags
- tape
- hole punch

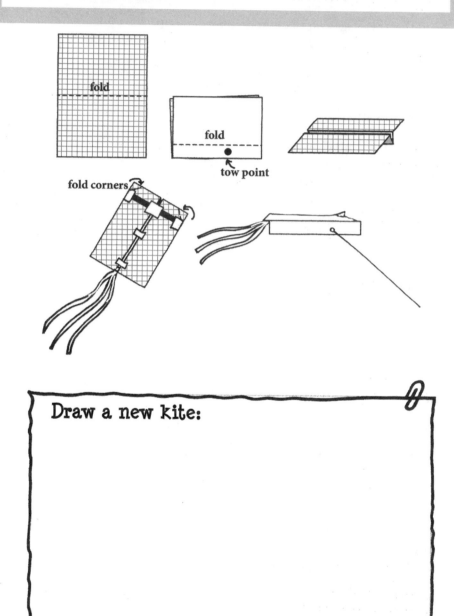

Draw a new kite:

# INCENTIVE PUBLICATIONS DAILY PRACTICE SERIES
## GRADE 6 MATH SKILLS

## Number Concepts

| Skill | 1 | 2 | 3 | 4 | 5 | 6 | 7 | 8 | 9 | 10 | 11 | 12 | 13 | 14 | 15 | 16 | 17 | 18 | 19 | 20 | 21 | 22 | 23 | 24 | 25 | 26 | 27 | 28 | 29 | 30 | 31 | 32 | 33 | 34 | 35 | 36 |
|---|---|---|---|---|---|---|---|---|---|---|---|---|---|---|---|---|---|---|---|---|---|---|---|---|---|---|---|---|---|---|---|---|---|---|---|---|
| Whole numbers: read, write, compare, order | ✓ |  | ✓ | ✓ | ✓ | ✓ | ✓ | ✓ | ✓ | ✓ | ✓ | ✓ | ✓ | ✓ | ✓ | ✓ | ✓ | ✓ | ✓ |  | ✓ | ✓ | ✓ | ✓ | ✓ | ✓ | ✓ | ✓ | ✓ | ✓ | ✓ | ✓ | ✓ | ✓ | ✓ | ✓ |
| Whole numbers: place value | ✓ | ✓ |  |  | ✓ |  | ✓ | ✓ |  |  | ✓ |  |  |  | ✓ | ✓ | ✓ |  | ✓ | ✓ |  |  |  |  |  |  |  |  |  |  | ✓ |  |  | ✓ |  |  |
| Whole numbers: rounding |  |  | ✓ | ✓ | ✓ | ✓ | ✓ | ✓ | ✓ |  | ✓ | ✓ |  |  |  |  |  | ✓ |  |  |  | ✓ |  |  |  |  | ✓ |  |  |  |  |  | ✓ |  | ✓ |  |
| Multiples, CM, LCM |  | ✓ | ✓ |  | ✓ |  |  |  | ✓ | ✓ |  |  |  | ✓ |  |  |  |  | ✓ | ✓ |  |  |  |  | ✓ |  |  |  |  | ✓ |  |  |  |  |  | ✓ |
| Factors, CF, GCF | ✓ | ✓ | ✓ |  | ✓ | ✓ | ✓ |  | ✓ |  |  |  | ✓ |  |  |  |  |  |  |  |  | ✓ |  |  |  |  |  |  | ✓ | ✓ |  |  |  |  |  |  |
| Divisibility | ✓ |  | ✓ |  | ✓ |  | ✓ |  |  |  | ✓ |  | ✓ |  | ✓ |  | ✓ | ✓ |  |  |  | ✓ |  | ✓ |  | ✓ |  |  | ✓ | ✓ |  |  | ✓ |  |  |  |
| Exponential numbers; scientific notation |  | ✓ |  |  |  | ✓ |  | ✓ |  | ✓ |  |  |  |  |  |  | ✓ |  |  |  | ✓ |  |  |  |  | ✓ |  | ✓ |  |  |  | ✓ |  | ✓ |  |  |
| Roots and radicals |  |  |  |  |  |  |  |  |  |  |  |  |  |  | ✓ | ✓ | ✓ | ✓ |  |  |  |  |  |  |  |  |  |  |  |  | ✓ |  |  |  |  |  |
| Fractions: read, write, compare, order | ✓ |  |  | ✓ | ✓ | ✓ | ✓ | ✓ | ✓ | ✓ | ✓ | ✓ | ✓ | ✓ | ✓ | ✓ | ✓ | ✓ | ✓ | ✓ | ✓ | ✓ | ✓ | ✓ | ✓ | ✓ | ✓ | ✓ | ✓ | ✓ | ✓ | ✓ | ✓ | ✓ | ✓ | ✓ |
| Fractions: rounding |  | ✓ |  |  |  |  |  |  | ✓ |  |  |  | ✓ | ✓ | ✓ | ✓ | ✓ |  |  |  |  |  | ✓ | ✓ | ✓ | ✓ | ✓ |  |  | ✓ |  |  | ✓ |  |  |  |
| Equivalent fractions |  |  |  |  |  |  | ✓ | ✓ |  |  | ✓ |  | ✓ |  | ✓ | ✓ |  |  |  |  |  | ✓ |  |  |  |  | ✓ | ✓ | ✓ | ✓ | ✓ |  |  | ✓ |  | ✓ |  |
| Fractions in lowest terms | ✓ | ✓ |  |  | ✓ | ✓ | ✓ |  | ✓ |  | ✓ | ✓ | ✓ |  | ✓ |  | ✓ | ✓ | ✓ | ✓ | ✓ | ✓ | ✓ | ✓ |  | ✓ | ✓ | ✓ |  | ✓ | ✓ | ✓ | ✓ | ✓ | ✓ |  |
| Ratios |  |  |  | ✓ | ✓ | ✓ | ✓ | ✓ | ✓ | ✓ | ✓ | ✓ | ✓ | ✓ | ✓ | ✓ | ✓ | ✓ | ✓ | ✓ | ✓ | ✓ | ✓ | ✓ | ✓ | ✓ | ✓ | ✓ | ✓ | ✓ | ✓ | ✓ | ✓ | ✓ | ✓ | ✓ |
| Proportions | ✓ | ✓ |  |  | ✓ | ✓ | ✓ |  | ✓ |  | ✓ | ✓ | ✓ |  | ✓ | ✓ | ✓ | ✓ | ✓ | ✓ | ✓ | ✓ | ✓ | ✓ | ✓ | ✓ | ✓ | ✓ | ✓ | ✓ | ✓ | ✓ | ✓ | ✓ | ✓ | ✓ |
| Decimals: read, write, compare, order | ✓ | ✓ | ✓ | ✓ | ✓ | ✓ | ✓ | ✓ | ✓ | ✓ | ✓ | ✓ | ✓ | ✓ | ✓ | ✓ | ✓ | ✓ | ✓ | ✓ | ✓ | ✓ | ✓ | ✓ | ✓ | ✓ | ✓ | ✓ | ✓ | ✓ | ✓ | ✓ | ✓ | ✓ | ✓ | ✓ |
| Decimals: rounding |  |  |  | ✓ | ✓ |  | ✓ | ✓ |  |  |  | ✓ | ✓ | ✓ |  |  |  |  | ✓ | ✓ | ✓ | ✓ | ✓ |  | ✓ |  |  |  | ✓ | ✓ |  |  |  |  |  | ✓ |
| Percent |  | ✓ |  | ✓ | ✓ | ✓ | ✓ | ✓ | ✓ |  | ✓ | ✓ | ✓ | ✓ | ✓ | ✓ | ✓ | ✓ | ✓ | ✓ | ✓ | ✓ | ✓ | ✓ | ✓ | ✓ | ✓ | ✓ | ✓ | ✓ | ✓ | ✓ | ✓ | ✓ | ✓ | ✓ |
| Fractions, decimals, percent relationships | ✓ |  | ✓ | ✓ | ✓ |  |  | ✓ |  |  |  |  |  | ✓ | ✓ |  |  | ✓ |  |  | ✓ | ✓ |  |  | ✓ | ✓ | ✓ |  |  | ✓ |  |  | ✓ |  | ✓ | ✓ |
| Money | ✓ | ✓ | ✓ | ✓ | ✓ | ✓ | ✓ | ✓ | ✓ |  | ✓ | ✓ | ✓ | ✓ | ✓ | ✓ | ✓ | ✓ | ✓ | ✓ | ✓ | ✓ | ✓ | ✓ | ✓ | ✓ | ✓ | ✓ | ✓ | ✓ | ✓ | ✓ | ✓ | ✓ | ✓ | ✓ |

113

# INCENTIVE PUBLICATIONS DAILY PRACTICE SERIES
## GRADE 6 · MATH SKILLS

## Operations/Computations

| Skill | 1 | 2 | 3 | 4 | 5 | 6 | 7 | 8 | 9 | 10 | 11 | 12 | 13 | 14 | 15 | 16 | 17 | 18 | 19 | 20 | 21 | 22 | 23 | 24 | 25 | 26 | 27 | 28 | 29 | 30 | 31 | 32 | 33 | 34 | 35 | 36 |
|---|---|---|---|---|---|---|---|---|---|---|---|---|---|---|---|---|---|---|---|---|---|---|---|---|---|---|---|---|---|---|---|---|---|---|---|---|
| Properties | ✓ | ✓ | ✓ | ✓ | | | | | | | | | | | | | | | | ✓ | | | | ✓ | ✓ | | | | | | ✓ | | | ✓ | | ✓ |
| Order of operations | | | ✓ | | | ✓ | | | | | | | | | | | | | | | | ✓ | ✓ | | | ✓ | | | ✓ | ✓ | ✓ | | ✓ | | | |
| Add and subtract whole numbers | ✓ | ✓ | ✓ | ✓ | | ✓ | | ✓ | ✓ | | | | ✓ | ✓ | | ✓ | ✓ | ✓ | ✓ | | ✓ | ✓ | | | | | ✓ | | ✓ | | | ✓ | | ✓ | | ✓ |
| Multiply whole numbers | ✓ | ✓ | | | | ✓ | ✓ | | ✓ | | | ✓ | ✓ | | ✓ | ✓ | ✓ | ✓ | | | | ✓ | | ✓ | ✓ | | ✓ | | ✓ | ✓ | | ✓ | | ✓ | ✓ | ✓ |
| Divide whole numbers | ✓ | ✓ | | | | | | | | ✓ | ✓ | ✓ | ✓ | ✓ | ✓ | ✓ | | ✓ | | ✓ | | ✓ | ✓ | | | | ✓ | | ✓ | ✓ | | ✓ | | ✓ | | ✓ |
| Multiply and divide with multiples of 10 | | | | ✓ | | | ✓ | | | | ✓ | | | ✓ | | ✓ | | | ✓ | | | | | | ✓ | | | | ✓ | | ✓ | | | | | |
| Averages | ✓ | | | | | | | | ✓ | | ✓ | | ✓ | | ✓ | | | | | ✓ | | | ✓ | ✓ | | ✓ | ✓ | ✓ | ✓ | | | ✓ | ✓ | | | ✓ |
| Add and subtract fractions | | | ✓ | ✓ | | ✓ | ✓ | ✓ | ✓ | | ✓ | | | | | | ✓ | | | | | ✓ | | | ✓ | | | | | | | | | | ✓ | |
| Multiply fractions | ✓ | | | | ✓ | ✓ | | ✓ | | | | | | ✓ | | | ✓ | | ✓ | ✓ | | | | | | | ✓ | ✓ | ✓ | ✓ | | | ✓ | | | ✓ |
| Divide fractions | | | | | ✓ | | | | | | | | | | | ✓ | | | | | | | | | | | | ✓ | | | | | | | | |
| Add and subtract decimals | ✓ | ✓ | ✓ | | | | ✓ | ✓ | ✓ | ✓ | | ✓ | ✓ | ✓ | ✓ | ✓ | ✓ | ✓ | | ✓ | ✓ | ✓ | ✓ | ✓ | ✓ | | ✓ | | ✓ | ✓ | | | | ✓ | | ✓ |
| Multiply decimals | ✓ | ✓ | ✓ | ✓ | | ✓ | ✓ | ✓ | ✓ | ✓ | ✓ | ✓ | ✓ | ✓ | ✓ | ✓ | | ✓ | ✓ | ✓ | | ✓ | ✓ | ✓ | ✓ | ✓ | ✓ | | ✓ | ✓ | | ✓ | ✓ | ✓ | ✓ | ✓ |
| Divide decimals | ✓ | ✓ | ✓ | ✓ | | | | | | ✓ | | ✓ | ✓ | ✓ | ✓ | ✓ | ✓ | | | | | | ✓ | ✓ | ✓ | ✓ | ✓ | ✓ | ✓ | ✓ | | | | ✓ | ✓ | ✓ |
| Operations with money | ✓ | ✓ | ✓ | ✓ | | ✓ | ✓ | ✓ | ✓ | ✓ | ✓ | | ✓ | | | ✓ | | ✓ | | ✓ | | | | | | | | ✓ | | ✓ | | | | | | |
| Add integers | ✓ | ✓ | ✓ | | | | | | | | | | | | | | ✓ | | | | | | | | | | | | ✓ | | | | | | | |
| Subtract integers | ✓ | ✓ | | | | | ✓ | | | | | | | | ✓ | | | ✓ | ✓ | | ✓ | ✓ | ✓ | ✓ | ✓ | ✓ | | | ✓ | | | | | ✓ | ✓ | |
| Multiply integers | | | ✓ | | ✓ | | | | ✓ | | | ✓ | ✓ | | ✓ | | | ✓ | ✓ | | ✓ | ✓ | | | | ✓ | | | ✓ | | | | | | | |
| Divide integers | | | | | | | | | | | | | | | | | | | | | | | | | | | | | ✓ | | | | | | | |
| Compute with roots, radicals, or exponents | | | ✓ | | | | | | | | | | | | | | | | | | | | | | | | | | | | | ✓ | | ✓ | | |
| Estimate answers | ✓ | ✓ | | ✓ | | | | ✓ | | | | ✓ | ✓ | ✓ | | ✓ | ✓ | ✓ | ✓ | ✓ | | ✓ | | ✓ | ✓ | ✓ | | ✓ | ✓ | | | ✓ | | | ✓ | ✓ |
| Find missing operation | | | | | | | | | | | | | | | | | | | | | | ✓ | | | | | | | | | | | | | | |
| Verify accuracy of computations | | | | | | | | | ✓ | | | | | ✓ | | | | | | | | | | | | ✓ | ✓ | ✓ | ✓ | | | ✓ | ✓ | | | ✓ |

114

©2006 Incentive Publications, Inc., Nashville, TN

# INCENTIVE PUBLICATIONS DAILY PRACTICE SERIES
## GRADE 6 MATH SKILLS

## Problem Solving

| Skill | 1 | 2 | 3 | 4 | 5 | 6 | 7 | 8 | 9 | 10 | 11 | 12 | 13 | 14 | 15 | 16 | 17 | 18 | 19 | 20 | 21 | 22 | 23 | 24 | 25 | 26 | 27 | 28 | 29 | 30 | 31 | 32 | 33 | 34 | 35 | 36 |
|---|---|---|---|---|---|---|---|---|---|---|---|---|---|---|---|---|---|---|---|---|---|---|---|---|---|---|---|---|---|---|---|---|---|---|---|---|
| Identify problem | ✓ | ✓ | ✓ |  |  | ✓ | ✓ | ✓ | ✓ |  | ✓ | ✓ |  |  |  |  |  |  |  |  |  |  | ✓ |  | ✓ |  |  | ✓ | ✓ | ✓ | ✓ | ✓ | ✓ | ✓ |  | ✓ |
| Necessary information | ✓ | ✓ | ✓ |  |  | ✓ | ✓ |  | ✓ |  |  | ✓ | ✓ |  |  |  |  |  |  | ✓ |  |  |  | ✓ | ✓ |  |  | ✓ | ✓ | ✓ |  |  | ✓ | ✓ |  |  |
| Necessary operations; order of operations | ✓ |  | ✓ | ✓ |  | ✓ |  |  |  |  |  |  |  |  |  | ✓ | ✓ |  | ✓ | ✓ | ✓ | ✓ | ✓ | ✓ |  | ✓ |  |  | ✓ |  | ✓ |  | ✓ |  |  | ✓ |
| Choose or explain strategy | ✓ | ✓ | ✓ | ✓ |  | ✓ | ✓ | ✓ | ✓ | ✓ | ✓ | ✓ |  |  | ✓ |  |  |  |  | ✓ |  |  |  |  | ✓ | ✓ |  |  |  |  | ✓ | ✓ |  |  |  | ✓ |
| Translate into an equation | ✓ | ✓ | ✓ | ✓ |  | ✓ |  |  | ✓ | ✓ | ✓ | ✓ |  |  |  | ✓ |  |  |  |  |  |  | ✓ | ✓ |  |  |  |  |  |  |  |  |  |  |  | ✓ |
| Extend a pattern | ✓ | ✓ | ✓ |  |  |  | ✓ | ✓ | ✓ | ✓ | ✓ | ✓ | ✓ |  | ✓ | ✓ |  |  |  | ✓ | ✓ |  | ✓ | ✓ |  | ✓ |  |  |  |  |  | ✓ |  |  |  | ✓ |
| Use a formula | ✓ | ✓ | ✓ | ✓ |  |  | ✓ | ✓ | ✓ | ✓ | ✓ | ✓ | ✓ |  | ✓ | ✓ | ✓ | ✓ |  | ✓ | ✓ | ✓ | ✓ |  | ✓ | ✓ | ✓ |  |  |  | ✓ | ✓ | ✓ | ✓ |  |  |
| Use diagrams/illustrations | ✓ | ✓ | ✓ |  | ✓ |  |  |  | ✓ |  | ✓ |  |  |  |  |  |  |  |  | ✓ |  |  |  |  | ✓ | ✓ |  |  |  |  | ✓ | ✓ |  | ✓ |  | ✓ |
| Use estimation | ✓ | ✓ |  | ✓ |  |  | ✓ |  |  |  |  |  |  |  |  |  |  |  |  |  |  |  |  |  |  |  |  |  |  |  |  |  |  |  | ✓ |  |
| Use mental math | ✓ | ✓ | ✓ |  |  |  |  |  | ✓ | ✓ | ✓ |  |  |  | ✓ | ✓ | ✓ | ✓ | ✓ | ✓ | ✓ | ✓ | ✓ |  | ✓ | ✓ | ✓ | ✓ | ✓ | ✓ | ✓ | ✓ | ✓ |  | ✓ |  |
| Use logic | ✓ | ✓ | ✓ | ✓ | ✓ | ✓ | ✓ | ✓ | ✓ | ✓ | ✓ | ✓ | ✓ | ✓ | ✓ | ✓ | ✓ | ✓ | ✓ | ✓ | ✓ | ✓ | ✓ | ✓ | ✓ | ✓ | ✓ | ✓ | ✓ | ✓ | ✓ | ✓ | ✓ | ✓ |  |  |
| Use trial and error | ✓ |  |  |  |  |  |  |  |  | ✓ |  |  |  |  |  |  |  |  |  |  |  |  |  |  |  |  |  |  |  |  |  |  |  |  |  |  |
| Use a graph or table | ✓ | ✓ | ✓ | ✓ | ✓ | ✓ | ✓ | ✓ | ✓ | ✓ |  | ✓ |  |  | ✓ | ✓ | ✓ | ✓ | ✓ |  | ✓ |  | ✓ | ✓ | ✓ | ✓ |  | ✓ |  | ✓ | ✓ | ✓ | ✓ | ✓ |  | ✓ |
| Set up a proportion | ✓ | ✓ | ✓ | ✓ | ✓ | ✓ | ✓ | ✓ | ✓ | ✓ |  |  | ✓ |  | ✓ | ✓ | ✓ | ✓ | ✓ | ✓ |  | ✓ | ✓ |  | ✓ | ✓ | ✓ | ✓ |  | ✓ |  | ✓ |  |  |  |  |
| Problems w/ whole numbers | ✓ | ✓ | ✓ | ✓ | ✓ | ✓ | ✓ | ✓ | ✓ | ✓ | ✓ | ✓ | ✓ | ✓ | ✓ | ✓ | ✓ | ✓ | ✓ | ✓ | ✓ | ✓ | ✓ | ✓ | ✓ | ✓ | ✓ | ✓ | ✓ | ✓ | ✓ | ✓ | ✓ | ✓ |  | ✓ |
| Problems w/ fractions | ✓ | ✓ | ✓ | ✓ | ✓ | ✓ | ✓ | ✓ | ✓ | ✓ | ✓ | ✓ | ✓ | ✓ | ✓ | ✓ | ✓ | ✓ | ✓ | ✓ | ✓ | ✓ | ✓ | ✓ | ✓ | ✓ | ✓ | ✓ | ✓ | ✓ | ✓ | ✓ | ✓ | ✓ | ✓ | ✓ |
| Problems w/ decimals | ✓ | ✓ | ✓ | ✓ | ✓ | ✓ | ✓ | ✓ | ✓ | ✓ | ✓ | ✓ | ✓ | ✓ | ✓ | ✓ | ✓ | ✓ | ✓ | ✓ | ✓ | ✓ | ✓ | ✓ | ✓ | ✓ | ✓ | ✓ | ✓ | ✓ | ✓ | ✓ | ✓ | ✓ | ✓ | ✓ |
| Problems w/ percent | ✓ | ✓ | ✓ | ✓ | ✓ | ✓ | ✓ | ✓ | ✓ | ✓ | ✓ | ✓ | ✓ | ✓ | ✓ |  |  | ✓ | ✓ | ✓ | ✓ | ✓ | ✓ | ✓ | ✓ | ✓ | ✓ | ✓ | ✓ | ✓ | ✓ | ✓ | ✓ | ✓ | ✓ | ✓ |
| Problems w/ roots, radicals, or exponents |  |  | ✓ |  |  | ✓ | ✓ |  | ✓ |  |  |  |  |  |  |  |  |  |  | ✓ |  |  |  |  |  |  |  |  |  |  |  | ✓ |  | ✓ |  |  |
| Problems w/ positive and negative numbers | ✓ |  |  | ✓ | ✓ | ✓ | ✓ | ✓ | ✓ | ✓ | ✓ | ✓ | ✓ | ✓ | ✓ | ✓ | ✓ | ✓ | ✓ | ✓ | ✓ | ✓ | ✓ | ✓ | ✓ | ✓ | ✓ | ✓ | ✓ | ✓ | ✓ | ✓ | ✓ | ✓ | ✓ | ✓ |
| Problems w/ rate or ratio | ✓ |  |  |  | ✓ | ✓ | ✓ | ✓ | ✓ | ✓ | ✓ |  | ✓ | ✓ | ✓ | ✓ | ✓ | ✓ |  | ✓ | ✓ | ✓ | ✓ |  |  |  |  | ✓ | ✓ |  |  | ✓ |  | ✓ | ✓ | ✓ |
| Problems w/ money | ✓ | ✓ |  | ✓ | ✓ | ✓ | ✓ | ✓ | ✓ | ✓ | ✓ | ✓ | ✓ | ✓ | ✓ | ✓ | ✓ | ✓ | ✓ | ✓ | ✓ | ✓ | ✓ | ✓ | ✓ | ✓ | ✓ | ✓ | ✓ | ✓ | ✓ | ✓ | ✓ | ✓ | ✓ | ✓ |
| Problems w/ time |  | ✓ |  | ✓ | ✓ | ✓ | ✓ | ✓ | ✓ | ✓ | ✓ | ✓ | ✓ | ✓ | ✓ | ✓ | ✓ | ✓ | ✓ | ✓ | ✓ | ✓ | ✓ | ✓ | ✓ | ✓ | ✓ | ✓ | ✓ | ✓ | ✓ | ✓ | ✓ | ✓ | ✓ | ✓ |
| Problems w/ measurement | ✓ | ✓ | ✓ | ✓ | ✓ | ✓ | ✓ | ✓ | ✓ | ✓ | ✓ | ✓ | ✓ | ✓ | ✓ | ✓ | ✓ | ✓ | ✓ | ✓ | ✓ | ✓ | ✓ | ✓ | ✓ | ✓ | ✓ | ✓ | ✓ | ✓ | ✓ | ✓ | ✓ | ✓ | ✓ | ✓ |
| Problems w/statistics | ✓ |  | ✓ |  | ✓ | ✓ |  |  |  | ✓ | ✓ |  |  |  |  | ✓ |  |  |  | ✓ |  | ✓ | ✓ | ✓ |  |  |  |  |  |  |  |  |  |  |  |  |
| Problems w/probability | ✓ |  |  |  |  |  |  |  |  | ✓ | ✓ |  | ✓ |  |  | ✓ | ✓ |  |  |  |  |  | ✓ |  |  |  | ✓ |  |  |  |  |  |  |  | ✓ |  |
| Open-ended problems |  |  |  | ✓ |  |  | ✓ |  |  |  |  |  |  |  |  |  |  | ✓ |  |  |  |  |  |  | ✓ |  | ✓ |  | ✓ |  |  |  |  |  |  |  |
| Reasonableness or accuracy of solutions | ✓ |  | ✓ | ✓ |  | ✓ | ✓ |  | ✓ | ✓ |  | ✓ |  | ✓ | ✓ | ✓ |  | ✓ | ✓ |  |  | ✓ | ✓ |  | ✓ | ✓ | ✓ | ✓ | ✓ | ✓ | ✓ | ✓ | ✓ | ✓ | ✓ | ✓ |

115

©2006 Incentive Publications, Inc., Nashville, TN

# INCENTIVE PUBLICATIONS DAILY PRACTICE SERIES
## GRADE 6 MATH SKILLS

### Geometry

| Skill | 1 | 2 | 3 | 4 | 5 | 6 | 7 | 8 | 9 | 10 | 11 | 12 | 13 | 14 | 15 | 16 | 17 | 18 | 19 | 20 | 21 | 22 | 23 | 24 | 25 | 26 | 27 | 28 | 29 | 30 | 31 | 32 | 33 | 34 | 35 | 36 |
|---|---|---|---|---|---|---|---|---|---|---|---|---|---|---|---|---|---|---|---|---|---|---|---|---|---|---|---|---|---|---|---|---|---|---|---|---|
| Points, lines, line segments, rays, and planes | | | | | | | | | | | | | | | | | | | | | | | | | | | | | | | | | ✓ | | | |
| Angles | | | | | ✓ | ✓ | ✓ | ✓ | ✓ | | | | | | ✓ | | | | | ✓ | | ✓ | | | ✓ | | | ✓ | ✓ | | ✓ | | ✓ | ✓ | | |
| Identify plane figures | ✓ | | ✓ | ✓ | | | | | | | | ✓ | ✓ | | | ✓ | | | ✓ | | | ✓ | ✓ | | | ✓ | | ✓ | | | ✓ | ✓ | | | | ✓ |
| Properties of plane figures | ✓ | | ✓ | | | | ✓ | | | ✓ | ✓ | ✓ | ✓ | | | ✓ | ✓ | | ✓ | | | ✓ | | | | ✓ | | | | | | ✓ | | | | ✓ |
| Symmetry | | | | | | | | ✓ | | ✓ | ✓ | | | | | | | | | | | | | ✓ | | | | | | | | ✓ | | | | |
| Identify space figures | ✓ | | ✓ | | | | | | | ✓ | | | | | | | | | | | ✓ | | | | | | | | | | | | | | | |
| Properties of space figures | ✓ | | | | | | | | | | | | | | | | | | | | | ✓ | | | | | | | ✓ | | | | | | | |
| Similar figures | | | | ✓ | | ✓ | | | | | | | | | | | | ✓ | | | | | | | | | ✓ | ✓ | ✓ | ✓ | | | | | | |
| Congruent figures and angles | | | | ✓ | | ✓ | | | ✓ | | | | | | | | | ✓ | | | | ✓ | | | | | ✓ | ✓ | ✓ | ✓ | | | | | | |
| Draw figures | | | | | ✓ | | ✓ | | | | | | | | | | | | | | | | | | ✓ | | | | | | | | | | ✓ | ✓ |

### Measurement

| Skill | 1 | 2 | 3 | 4 | 5 | 6 | 7 | 8 | 9 | 10 | 11 | 12 | 13 | 14 | 15 | 16 | 17 | 18 | 19 | 20 | 21 | 22 | 23 | 24 | 25 | 26 | 27 | 28 | 29 | 30 | 31 | 32 | 33 | 34 | 35 | 36 |
|---|---|---|---|---|---|---|---|---|---|---|---|---|---|---|---|---|---|---|---|---|---|---|---|---|---|---|---|---|---|---|---|---|---|---|---|---|
| Measurement units | ✓ | | | ✓ | ✓ | ✓ | ✓ | ✓ | ✓ | ✓ | | ✓ | ✓ | ✓ | | ✓ | ✓ | ✓ | ✓ | | | ✓ | | ✓ | ✓ | ✓ | ✓ | ✓ | ✓ | ✓ | | ✓ | | | ✓ | ✓ |
| Estimate measurements | | ✓ | | ✓ | | ✓ | ✓ | | ✓ | | | ✓ | | | | | ✓ | ✓ | | | | | | | | ✓ | | ✓ | | | | | | | | |
| Convert units | | | ✓ | ✓ | ✓ | ✓ | | ✓ | | | | ✓ | | | ✓ | ✓ | ✓ | ✓ | ✓ | | | ✓ | | ✓ | ✓ | ✓ | | | ✓ | ✓ | ✓ | | | | | ✓ |
| Angle measurements | | | | | ✓ | | | | ✓ | | | | | | | | ✓ | | | | | | | | | | | | | | | | | | | |
| Measure length | ✓ | | | | | | ✓ | | | ✓ | | | | | | ✓ | | | | ✓ | ✓ | ✓ | | | | | | ✓ | | ✓ | | | | | | |
| Choose correct formula | | | | ✓ | | | | | | ✓ | | ✓ | | | | ✓ | | | ✓ | | ✓ | | | | | | ✓ | | | ✓ | ✓ | | | | | |
| Perimeter, circumference | ✓ | | | | | | | | ✓ | ✓ | | ✓ | | | ✓ | ✓ | ✓ | | | ✓ | | | ✓ | ✓ | | | | ✓ | | ✓ | | | | | | ✓ |
| Area of plane figures | | | ✓ | | | | ✓ | ✓ | | | ✓ | | ✓ | ✓ | | | | ✓ | | | | | ✓ | ✓ | | ✓ | | ✓ | | | | | | | | |
| Surface area (space figures) | | | | | | | | | | | | | | | | | | | | ✓ | | | | | ✓ | | | | | | | | | | | |
| Volume of space figures | | | ✓ | | ✓ | | | | | | | | | | | | ✓ | | | | | | | | | | | ✓ | ✓ | ✓ | | | | | | |
| Temperature | ✓ | | | | | | | | | | | | | | | | | | | | | | | | | | | | | | | | | | | |
| Time | ✓ | | ✓ | ✓ | ✓ | ✓ | ✓ | ✓ | ✓ | ✓ | | ✓ | ✓ | | ✓ | | ✓ | ✓ | ✓ | ✓ | | ✓ | | ✓ | | | ✓ | ✓ | ✓ | ✓ | ✓ | | | ✓ | ✓ | ✓ |
| Weight | | | | | | ✓ | ✓ | ✓ | ✓ | | | | | | | | | | ✓ | | | | | | | | | | | | | | | ✓ | | |
| Scale | | | ✓ | | | | | | | | | | | ✓ | | | | ✓ | | | | | ✓ | | | | ✓ | | | | | | ✓ | | | ✓ |
| Reasonableness of a measurement | | | | ✓ | ✓ | ✓ | ✓ | ✓ | ✓ | | | | | | | | | | | ✓ | | ✓ | | ✓ | | | | ✓ | | | | | | | | |
| Compare measurements | ✓ | | | | | | | ✓ | | | | ✓ | | | | | | | | | | | | | ✓ | ✓ | ✓ | ✓ | ✓ | | | | ✓ | | | ✓ |

# INCENTIVE PUBLICATIONS DAILY PRACTICE SERIES
## GRADE 6 MATH SKILLS

## Statistics & Graphing

| Skill | 1 | 2 | 3 | 4 | 5 | 6 | 7 | 8 | 9 | 10 | 11 | 12 | 13 | 14 | 15 | 16 | 17 | 18 | 19 | 20 | 21 | 22 | 23 | 24 | 25 | 26 | 27 | 28 | 29 | 30 | 31 | 32 | 33 | 34 | 35 | 36 |
|---|---|---|---|---|---|---|---|---|---|---|---|---|---|---|---|---|---|---|---|---|---|---|---|---|---|---|---|---|---|---|---|---|---|---|---|---|
| Define statistical terms | | | ✓ | | | | ✓ | | | ✓ | | | | | | | | | | | | ✓ | | | | | | | | | | | | | | |
| Interpret tables | ✓ | ✓ | ✓ | ✓ | ✓ | ✓ | | ✓ | | | ✓ | ✓ | | ✓ | | ✓ | ✓ | ✓ | ✓ | ✓ | ✓ | | ✓ | ✓ | ✓ | ✓ | ✓ | ✓ | ✓ | | ✓ | ✓ | ✓ | ✓ | ✓ | ✓ |
| Find mean, range, median, mode in a set of data | ✓ | | ✓ | | | | | | ✓ | | ✓ | | ✓ | | ✓ | ✓ | ✓ | ✓ | ✓ | | ✓ | ✓ | ✓ | ✓ | ✓ | ✓ | ✓ | ✓ | ✓ | ✓ | | | ✓ | | | |
| Select appropriate graph | | | | | | | | | | | | | | | | | ✓ | ✓ | | | | ✓ | | | | ✓ | | | | | | | ✓ | | | |
| Interpret graphs | | ✓ | | | ✓ | ✓ | ✓ | | | | | ✓ | | | ✓ | | | | | | ✓ | ✓ | | | ✓ | | | | ✓ | | ✓ | | | | | ✓ |
| Solve problems from data | ✓ | | ✓ | ✓ | | | | | ✓ | | ✓ | ✓ | | | | ✓ | ✓ | ✓ | ✓ | ✓ | ✓ | ✓ | | | | | ✓ | ✓ | | | ✓ | | ✓ | ✓ | ✓ | ✓ |
| Translate data into a graph or table | ✓ | | ✓ | ✓ | ✓ | | ✓ | ✓ | ✓ | | ✓ | | ✓ | | | | | | ✓ | | | ✓ | | ✓ | | | ✓ | | ✓ | | | ✓ | | ✓ | | ✓ |
| Coordinate graphs | | | | | | ✓ | | | | | | | ✓ | ✓ | | | | ✓ | | | | | ✓ | | ✓ | | | ✓ | | | | | | | | |

## Probability

| Skill | 1 | 2 | 3 | 4 | 5 | 6 | 7 | 8 | 9 | 10 | 11 | 12 | 13 | 14 | 15 | 16 | 17 | 18 | 19 | 20 | 21 | 22 | 23 | 24 | 25 | 26 | 27 | 28 | 29 | 30 | 31 | 32 | 33 | 34 | 35 | 36 |
|---|---|---|---|---|---|---|---|---|---|---|---|---|---|---|---|---|---|---|---|---|---|---|---|---|---|---|---|---|---|---|---|---|---|---|---|---|
| Define probability terms | ✓ | ✓ | ✓ | ✓ | | | | | | | | | | | | | | | | | | | | | | | | | | | | | | | | |
| Describe likelihood of an event | ✓ | | | ✓ | | ✓ | ✓ | ✓ | | | ✓ | | ✓ | | ✓ | | | | ✓ | ✓ | ✓ | ✓ | | ✓ | ✓ | ✓ | | | ✓ | | | ✓ | ✓ | | ✓ | |
| Outcomes of one event | | | | ✓ | ✓ | ✓ | | ✓ | ✓ | | | | ✓ | | | | | | | ✓ | ✓ | | | ✓ | | | | | | ✓ | ✓ | | | | | |
| Probability of one event | | | | | ✓ | ✓ | | ✓ | ✓ | | | | ✓ | | | | ✓ | | ✓ | ✓ | ✓ | | | ✓ | | ✓ | ✓ | | ✓ | ✓ | | | ✓ | | ✓ | ✓ |
| Outcomes of two independent events | | | | | | | | ✓ | | | | | | | | | | | | | | | | | | | ✓ | | | | | | | ✓ | | |
| Tree diagrams | ✓ | | | | | | | | | | ✓ | | | | ✓ | | | ✓ | | | | | | | | | | | | | | | ✓ | | | |
| Probability of two independent events | | | | | | | | ✓ | | | | | | | | | | ✓ | | | | | | | | | ✓ | | | | | | | ✓ | | |
| Outcomes/probability of two dependent events | | | | | | | | | | | | | | | ✓ | ✓ | ✓ | ✓ | | | | | | | | | | | | ✓ | | | | | | |
| Combinations and permutations | | | | | | | | | | | ✓ | | | ✓ | ✓ | | | | | | | | ✓ | | | | | | | | | | | ✓ | | |
| Odds for or against | | | | | | | | | | | | | | ✓ | ✓ | ✓ | | | | | | | | | | | | ✓ | | | | | | | | |

Use It! Don't Lose It! IP 613-1

117

# INCENTIVE PUBLICATIONS DAILY PRACTICE SERIES
# GRADE 6 MATH SKILLS

## Pre-Algebra

| Skill | 1 | 2 | 3 | 4 | 5 | 6 | 7 | 8 | 9 | 10 | 11 | 12 | 13 | 14 | 15 | 16 | 17 | 18 | 19 | 20 | 21 | 22 | 23 | 24 | 25 | 26 | 27 | 28 | 29 | 30 | 31 | 32 | 33 | 34 | 35 | 36 |
|---|---|---|---|---|---|---|---|---|---|---|---|---|---|---|---|---|---|---|---|---|---|---|---|---|---|---|---|---|---|---|---|---|---|---|---|---|
| Patterns and functions | | √ | | | | | | | √ | √ | √ | √ | | √ | | √ | √ | | | | | | √ | √ | | √ | √ | | √ | √ | √ | | | | | √ |
| Opposites; absolute value | | | | | | | | | | | √ | | | | | | | | | √ | | | | | | | | | | | | | | | | |
| Compute with positive and negative numbers | √ | √ | √ | | | √ | √ | | | √ | √ | | √ | | √ | | √ | | √ | √ | √ | √ | √ | | √ | √ | | | | √ | √ | | √ | | | |
| Read and write expressions | | √ | √ | | | | | | √ | | √ | | | | | √ | √ | √ | | √ | | | | | √ | | | | | | | √ | | | | |
| Simplify expressions | | | | | | | | | | | √ | | | | √ | √ | √ | | | | | | √ | | √ | | √ | | | √ | √ | | | | | √ |
| Read, write, graph inequalities | | | | | √ | √ | √ | | | | | | | | | | | | √ | √ | √ | | √ | | | √ | | √ | √ | √ | √ | √ | | √ | | |
| Read and write equations | √ | √ | | √ | √ | | √ | √ | √ | √ | √ | √ | √ | | √ | | | √ | | | | | | | | √ | | | | √ | √ | √ | | | | |
| Match equations to problems | | | | √ | | | | | | | | | | | | | | | | | | | | | | | | | | | | | | | | |
| Simplify equations | | | | | | | | | √ | √ | | | | | | √ | | | | | | √ | | | | | √ | | | | | | √ | | | |
| Solve equations – one variable, one step | | | √ | | √ | √ | √ | √ | √ | √ | √ | √ | √ | √ | √ | √ | √ | √ | √ | √ | | √ | √ | | √ | | √ | √ | | √ | | | √ | | √ | √ |
| Solve equations – one variable, multiple steps | | | √ | | √ | √ | √ | √ | √ | √ | √ | | | | √ | | √ | √ | | √ | √ | √ | | | | | | | | √ | | | | | √ | √ |
| Solve equations with two variables; write solution sets | | | | | | | | | | | | | | | | √ | | | | | | | | | √ | | | | | | | | | | | |
| Order of operations in equations | | | | √ | | √ | √ | √ | | √ | √ | √ | √ | | | | | | | | | √ | | | | | | | | | | | √ | | | |
| Verify accuracy of solutions | √ | √ | | √ | | √ | √ | | | √ | √ | | √ | | | | | | | | | √ | | √ | √ | | | | | | | | √ | | | |

Use It! Don't Lose It! IP 613-1

## Week 1 (pages 5–7)

**MONDAY**
1. perimeter = 24 feet
2. 328
3. trapezoid
4. <
5. Each lunch includes 3 sandwiches, a bag of chips, an apple, 2 bottles of water, and a candy bar. Leftovers include: 7 bags of chips, 3 apples, 6 bottles of water, and 7 candy bars.

**TUESDAY**
1. 1,532,482 scouts & leaders
2. 8,000
3. Estimates will vary. There are fewer than two scouts for every leader.
4. 52°F
5. total = $277.54; average = $46.26

**WEDNESDAY**
1. 66 boxes, 4 more kits
2. 5 out of 8
3. 18
4. 59
5. a. 4, b. 2, c. 5, d. 1, e. 3

**THURSDAY**
1. 7 teams; 2 leaders and 11 scouts per team
2. 65 campers
3. on June 4
4. 2.7 cm.
5.
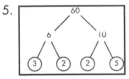

**FRIDAY**
1. 19 – (–10) = 29
2. 8 x 27 = total; 216 plants
3. 160,000
4. estimate: 49; difference: 49.21
5. a. Week 4
   b. increase by 13
   c. 360 pancakes

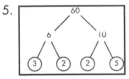

## Week 2 (pages 8–10)

**MONDAY**
1. commutative property
2. 546 steps; the number of steps is not equal.
3. 12:35 p.m.
4. $10.00 – $5.76 = change; $4.24
5. $41.50

**TUESDAY**
1. a. 31 tons copper
   b. 125 tons steel
   c. 27,000 tons concrete
2. a. 14      b. 19.2
3. yes
4. 6,004,030
5. a. 15 b. c = 6, a = 9, b = 3

**WEDNESDAY**
1. +2
2. a. 18"      b. 30"
3. 5
4. There is a 1 in 10 chance of rain.
5. a. 23 chaperones
   b. 3 hours (Students and chaperones will tour.)

**THURSDAY**
1. Answers will vary. In October, 2006, Lady Liberty was officially 120 years old.
2. An unknown quantity *t* divided by four plus one
3. One hundredth is equal to ten thousandths so 72 hundredths is equal to 72 x 10 hundredths or 720 thousandths. (.72 = .720)
4. 54"; answers will vary
5. 22x = $137.77; $6.26

**FRIDAY**
1. a. true; b. false; c. true
2. 8:28 a.m.
3. $\frac{6}{17}$
4. a. <; b. <; c. >
5.

## Week 3 (pages 11–13)

**MONDAY**
1. 23,700
2. twice the sum of 14 and a number
3. It means that out of 100 chances, the volcano will erupt 100 times.
4. a. 4 equal sides
   b. 4 equal angles
   c. opposite sides are parallel
5. a. Diagrams will vary. height = 1,079 feet
   b. Since most of the volcano's height is under sea level, the volcano is probably located on the ocean floor.

**TUESDAY**
1. 75%
2. associative property of addition
3. 25 years
4. 297 years
5. 8:05 a.m.

**WEDNESDAY**
1. x = 5
2. 64
3. 1, 9, 27, 3
4. a. parallelogram
   b. hexagon
   c. rectangle
   d. octagon
5. Change the hours to minutes and add the times together. Divide by 3.

**THURSDAY**
1. $3\frac{1}{16}$
2. The lava is 550° C hotter.
3. 8.2 ÷ 10
4. 336 pieces
5. a. 10,000; b. 5; c. 100,000; d. 6; e. 1,000,000
   The exponent equals the number of zeroes in the number written in standard form.

**FRIDAY**
1. It received a VEI of 5 and was called a paroxysmal eruption.
2. Huge eruptions do not seem to happen frequently.

3. Howard is incorrect. While the numbers appear to be smaller, Howard failed to look at the units. The volume of a cataclysmic volcano is reported in meters$^3$ and the volume of paroxysmal volcano is reported in kilometers$^3$. A kilometer represents 1000 meters.
4. 900,000,000 m$^3$
5. 200,960,000,000 ft$^3$

## Week 4 (pages 14–16)

**MONDAY**
1. zero property or the identity property
2. w = 20
3. 170,000
4. n = 18
5. $\frac{1}{2}$

**TUESDAY**
1. The two figures are congruent.
2. 134.8
3. square feet
4. 13 feet of doweling
5. 80 characters

**WEDNESDAY**
1. Definitions will vary. Probability is the likelihood something will occur.
2. No, it will take him 800 minutes.
3. step 9
4. Answers will vary. Some possible answers are –5, –4.5, –4.3. The answers are not all integers, because integers must be whole numbers.
5. a and d

**THURSDAY**
1. $\frac{9}{2} > \frac{5}{6}$
2. c x b = b x c
3. n = –12
4. $\frac{7}{8}$
5. c.

**FRIDAY**
1. 12' x 16' = 192 square feet
2. c.
3. b.
4. 0.14
5. a. about $53.00
   b. about $22.00
   c. about $3.00

# ANSWER KEY

## Week 5 (pages 17–19)

**MONDAY**

1. about 12,480 square miles
2. The value of the 7 is seven thousand.
3. a. A ratio is a comparison between two numbers or amounts, so for every iceberg there are five penguins.
   b. 30 penguins
4. a. composite, b. composite
5. a. more than 2,996 years;
   b. Conclusions will vary, but should reflect the enormous amount of time an iceberg takes to form versus the comparatively short time it takes to melt.

**TUESDAY**

1. Answers will vary. Two possible answers are 24 and 48.
2. 2.39 miles
3. 1.84
4. 34,079
5. a. Large; b. Growler; c. Small; d. Very Large

**WEDNESDAY**

1. c.
2. $\frac{4}{8}$ or $\frac{1}{2}$
3. 72
4. $\frac{3}{7}$
5. Diagrams will vary, but the iceberg diagrammed should have steep sides with a flat top and a length-height ratio of less than 5:1

**THURSDAY**

1. ruler
2. Tuesday
3. $\frac{36}{48}$ or $\frac{3}{4}$
4. January 12
5. a. True. The chart shows that 48.5% of the icebergs were of unknown size.
   b. False. Only 12.5% were classified as large and 2.8% were classified as very large—that's only about 30% of the classified icebergs.
   c. True. Small and medium

icebergs are more than 30% of the total number of icebergs, or about 60% of all icebergs.

**FRIDAY**

1. 706 passengers
2. 52 children
3. 215 crewmembers
4. about 32%
5.

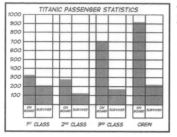

## Week 6 (pages 20–22)

**MONDAY**

1. 6,800,000
2. x = 19
3. 9,600 chocolate bars
4. 81 square inches
5. a. d and f      b. a and c

**TUESDAY**

1. 135%
2. a box of chocolates
3. $1,250.00
4. 736.4
5. a

**WEDNESDAY**

1. Estimates will vary. The angle is about 60 degrees.
2. intersecting lines
3. a. 3 possible outcomes
   b. red: 1 in 4 chance; pink: 1 in 2 chance
   c. Probably, but if the candies eaten included 6 red, 6 white, and 12 pink the odds would remain the same.
4. r = −13
5. a. (3, 4); b. (−3, 2); c. (−2, 5); d. (4, 6); e. (3, 1)

**THURSDAY**

1. $1\frac{7}{15}$
2. 14
3. c
4. a. 53, b. 25, 1.52
5. Charlie dropped four marshmallows.

**FRIDAY**

1. 13 batches
2. 3 gallons
3. 111 servings
4. 2 gross
5. 3 dozen eggs, 3 tins of cocoa, 1 bottle of vanilla, 3 boxes of butter, 1 bag of flour, 2 bags of sugar

## Week 7 (pages 23–25)

**MONDAY**

1. 7,644,000
2. y = 15
3. 11x = $110. The Pod cost $10.00.
4. $\frac{1}{2}$(10") x 5" = a (25 square inches)
5. a. mean, b. range, c. mode, d. median

**TUESDAY**

1. .06
2. b
3. $115.00
4. 736.4
5. a. 450 – 1,200 LEGOS
   b. 775 LEGOS

**WEDNESDAY**

1. a
2. c.
3. x = 72
4. $4 \times 10^{10}$
5. 6 in 11

**THURSDAY**

1. $1\frac{1}{3}$
2. $48.00
3. 75,600 sets
4. $3\frac{1}{2}$"
5. $\frac{6}{9} = \frac{20}{30}$, 20 black bricks

**FRIDAY**

1. $\frac{2}{3} < \frac{7}{9}$
2. $\frac{7}{9} < \frac{4}{5}$
3. $\frac{80}{100} = \frac{4}{5}$
4. 208,333,333 days
5. You need eight connectors to build a cube. Students should draw an accurate triangular prism and a rectangular prism. Six connectors are needed to build the triangular prism and eight connectors for the rectangular prism.

## Week 8 (pages 26–28)

**MONDAY**

1. $225.00
2. 20" x 25" = area; more
3. a. $\frac{3}{5}$, b. $\frac{2}{7}$, c. $\frac{2}{3}$
4. 3 and 4
5. 1 out of 25

**TUESDAY**

1. 40 GB
2. 1,155
3. $10^9$
4. eight hundred twenty-two millions + one hundred fifty thousands
5. two pounds less; 32 ounces

**WEDNESDAY**

1. 1 in 4
2. associative property of multiplication
3. $\frac{3}{8}$
4. 17 years and 11 months
5. parallel lines = a; perpendicular lines = b; intersecting lines = c

**THURSDAY**

1. $\frac{5}{12}$
2. feet and yards
3. 64
4. b = 27
5. three inches

**FRIDAY**

1. 223,810,000 PCs
2. 69,200,000 PCs
3. 154,610,000 PCs
4. 74,603,000 laptops
5. Circle graphs will vary slightly.

## Week 9 (pages 29–31)

**MONDAY**

1. x = 44
2. 560
3. $4\frac{1}{5}$ trips
4. 12 white ties
5. 25 square feet, 24 foot perimeter

**TUESDAY**

1. 4%
2. $58.14
3. 8' x 9'
4. c
5. b

## WEDNESDAY

1. a. $\frac{1}{\$6.75} = \frac{8}{x}$

   x = $54.00

   b. $\frac{3 \text{ feet}}{1 \text{ yard}} = \frac{x}{15 \text{ yards}}$

   x = 45 feet

   c. $\frac{9}{1} = \frac{x}{7}$

   x = 63 rungs
2. −41.85
3. x
4. 324; 972; 2,916
5. a. neither congruent nor similar
   b. neither congruent nor similar
   c. congruent
   d. neither congruent nor similar

## THURSDAY

1. $\frac{7}{12}$
2. x = 11.4
3. b
4. n($.35) = $14.70, n = 42
5. a. fruit; b. cheese; c. 5

## FRIDAY

1. 30″
2. 30″ x 40″ = 2′6″ x 3′4″ = $2\frac{1}{2}$ feet x $3\frac{1}{3}$ feet
3. yes
4. 225 square inches
5. Drawings will vary. Furniture items should be drawn to scale.

# Week 10 (pages 32–34)

## MONDAY

1. Students will estimate an answer of about 500. Actual answer is 512.
2. seven cans (6.857)
3. a. k + 10, b. 30n, c. $\frac{20}{r}$
4. cube
5. a. the amount in tons of waste produced per person per year
   b. .916 tons of waste per person per year
   c. .384 tons of waste per person per year; 768 pounds

## TUESDAY

1. 90,000,000,000 pounds or 90 x 10⁹
2. a. false, b. true, c. false
3. 6
4. 3,798,400 tons of waste
5. Two problems will be corrected.

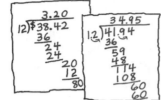

## WEDNESDAY

1. 36 shoeboxes
2. false
3. eight less than a number y
4. No. Explanations will vary, but should note that recycling 2,000 pounds of glass saves nine gallons of oil. The Avery farm uses 200 gallons of oil during the winter alone—or the equivalent of 22 tons of recycled glass. One farm probably does not use that much glass.
5. regular pentagon; 5(s) = perimeter; 11.25 cm.

## THURSDAY

1. 205 minutes
2. $5\frac{1}{4}$, 6, $6\frac{3}{4}$
   The pattern is $+\frac{3}{4}$.
3. c
4. 2.25 kg
5.

## FRIDAY

1. − 28
2. 60
3. 24 plants
4. x = .3
5. a. Fifteen days later the pick-ups will be on the day again. Explanations will vary. Marking the pickups on a blank calendar is one way to solve the problem.
   b. Two Mondays will pass, the pickup will be on the third Monday.

# Week 11 (pages 35–37)

## MONDAY

1. 500–600 offspring survive
2. a. 8 + k
   b. 10 − n
   c. h − 43
   d. 17m
3. a. 28, b. 6
4. 27
5. 32 square inches

## TUESDAY

1. n = 23.4
2. 14 spotted turtles
3. yes
4. The number of digits to the right of the product is the same as the sum of the digits to the right of the decimal place in the two factors.
5. 22.2 fish

## WEDNESDAY

1. a. −13; b. 8; c. −150
2. −3
3. h = 5.5(1.5 feet) or 8.25 ft
4. 18 times
5.

## THURSDAY

1. Answers will vary.
2. c
3. $15\frac{5}{6}$ yards
4. It will take the tortoise a 23.8 minutes.
5. 6 permutations possible:

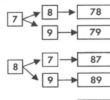

## FRIDAY

1. 3, 2, 16, 80, 400, 2,000, 10,000

2. 7.7436
3. a. 216      c. 261
   b. .222     d. 2.16
4. a. y = 29    c. a = 25
   b. n = 22    d. a = 19.4
5. One possible solution:

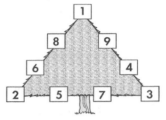

# Week 12 (pages 38–40)

## MONDAY

1. work force x 24 hours x 365 days = man-hours per year; 9,000 x 24 x 365 = 78,840,000 man-hours per year
2. 855,000
3. 18,867
4. 178,617
5. toll paid/length of the canal
   The Coral Princess paid $2,827.43 per kilometer. Richard Halliburton paid .45 of a cent, or $.0045 per kilometer.

## TUESDAY

1. 49.68 miles
2. 8.688
3. .4096
4. d.
5. 28,000 vessels

## WEDNESDAY

1. −5 > −3
2. about 30 kilometers per hour
3. a. 5,400, b. −25, c. −15
4. −1
5. Diagrams will vary. 26 m

## THURSDAY

1. 4
2. $2\frac{3}{8}$
3. Explanations will vary. The answer is $2\frac{1}{2}$.
4. Canal traffic averaged 11,383 vessels per year. It is not reasonable to think that the same number of vessels went through the canal in 1914 as did in

# ANSWER KEY

2005. International trade has changed dramatically.
5. No, the problem cannot be solved without knowing the number of American taxpayers.

### FRIDAY
1. false
2. false
3. true
4. true
5. 27.2%; graphs will vary.

## Week 13 (pages 41–43)

### MONDAY
1. about 2 years, 3 days
2. $176.00
3. 540,000 square feet
4. 1, 9, 3
5. $\frac{2}{9} = \frac{x}{48}$; $10\frac{2}{3}$ times

### TUESDAY
1. Distributive Property of Multiplication
2. $52.71
3. hexagon
4. 3.22
5. Sentences will vary.

### WEDNESDAY
1. Seven yards six inches
2. 7.065 square feet
3. 1 in 4 chance
4. x = 50
5. 72 uniforms

### THURSDAY
1. three tickets to Busch Stadium
2. b.
3. $3\frac{3}{4}$ pints
4. a. $\frac{2}{7}$;   b. $\frac{1}{3}$;   c. $\frac{4}{5}$
5. There are 42 people in the group. Explanations will vary.

### FRIDAY
Student choices for ballparks will vary, so answers will vary.

## Week 14 (pages 44–46)

### MONDAY
1. (–3, 2)
2.
```
   8,472
 x    38
  67776
  25416
 321,936
```

3. 8
4. 9
5. Facts marked are a., c., d., f., & g.

### TUESDAY
1. a. about 20; b. about $1; c. about $5
2. z = 2.2
3. 736
4. 70.005
5. 125 pounds

### WEDNESDAY
1. a. 10
   b. –5
   c. –21
2. a
3. –77, –7.7, .077, .770, 7, 70, 770
4. Answers will vary, but should reflect that the value of one dollar during the days of the Pony Express was fifteen times more than the value of one dollar today.
5. a. §   b. ▯▯▯   c. ⌘

### THURSDAY
1. 12 permutations
2. $\frac{5}{16}, \frac{7}{20}, \frac{17}{40}$
3. $\frac{9}{20}$
4. $7\frac{13}{24}$
5. $8\frac{3}{4}$"

### FRIDAY
1. about 35 stations
2. 5 horses
3. 70 miles
4. No, explanations will vary.
5. Created routes will vary.

## Week 15 (pages 47–49)

### MONDAY
1. a. yes; b. no; c. yes
2. AD || EF
3. 27,282,555
4. 3 cubed means 3 multiplied by itself twice. 3 x 3 x 3 = 81
5. a. 5 vegetables
   b. 4 vegetables
   c. No, explanations will vary.

### TUESDAY
1. 5

2. Six hours and 30 minutes; explanations will vary
3. 85% of 35
4. 20
5. Carlos gets paid $4.95 per hour. Marie gets paid $4.20 per hour. Together the weeders earn $9.15 per hour.

### WEDNESDAY
1. –10" She needs to dig 14" more.
2. 37.68 m
3. –20
4. There is one chance out of eleven that he will plant two pumpkin seeds in a row.
5.

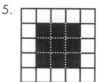

### THURSDAY
1. a. $\frac{7}{5}$ or $1\frac{2}{5}$; b. $\frac{9}{6}$ or $1\frac{1}{2}$; c. $\frac{15}{8}$ or $1\frac{7}{8}$
2. $\frac{5}{21}$
3. Area = 5,184 square inches or 36 square feet; Perimeter = 24 feet, 2 inches
4. c
5. eight ounces

### FRIDAY
1. a. 30 paving stones;
   b. $22.50
2. Three different color combinations: green and brown, green and cream, brown and cream
3. Patterns will vary.
4. Patterns will vary.
5. Designs will vary. Changing the shape does change the area

## Week 16 (pages 50–52)

### MONDAY
1. 2,619
2. c.
3. q = 24
4. quadrilateral, polygon, rectangle
5. The python weighs 262.5 pounds. Sentences will vary

but should reference the fact that while the pythons are longer, the anacondas are heavier.

### TUESDAY
1. 37.68"
2. 256.1
3. $46.01
4. 7"
5. a. median = 7
   b. 137 babies in all
   c. range = 4–10 babies

### WEDNESDAY
1. –20
2. –20 points
3. one
4. cylinder
5. 10–14°F

### THURSDAY
1. a. $\frac{3}{7}$; b. $\frac{3}{7}$; c. $\frac{1}{4}$
2. 90,000
3. b > 15
4. n > 22
5. 396 inches; Comparisons will vary.

### FRIDAY
1. a. $\frac{1}{2}$; b. $\frac{2}{3}$; c. $\frac{3}{4}$
2. a. > ; b. = ; c. <
3. x = 2.5
4. c = 5
5. Patterns will vary.

## Week 17 (pages 53–55)

### MONDAY
1. $35 \times 10^{7}$
2. c
3. (12 – 8) + (5 + 2) = 11
4. 9,002,000
5. No, you need to know the month the term was first used.

### TUESDAY
1. p = 40
2. about 20,800 times
3. a. Subtract 3.2 from 6.4.
   b. Multiply 0.3 by 10.
4. 0.008
5. $40.45

### WEDNESDAY
1. No, the chances of picking a particular shoe the first time are one in three. The chances of picking a matching shoe on the second pick are one in five.

2. a. + 35; b. –17; c. –7
3. –6
4. 260,000 pairs of shoes
5. The average falls between 8 and 9. 8.45   8

**THURSDAY**
1. Two million shoes
2. a. no; b. yes
3. $45.00
4. 58,398
5. $10\frac{1}{2}$ inches

**FRIDAY**
1. a = 44
2.
3. 164
4. three congruent sides—equilateral triangle; at least two congruent sides—isosceles triangle; no congruent sides—scalene triangle
5. Traci will pay $47.92. She would save $9.95 with UPS Ground.

# Week 18 (pages 56–58)

**MONDAY**
1. a. about 4,500 square miles; b. about 41%
2. population (1,211,537) ÷ land area (6,423) = population per square mile; 188.62478 or about 189 people per square mile
3. a. 7,049,004; seven million, forty-nine thousand, four
   b. 503,502; five hundred three thousand, five hundred two
4. 58,786
5. Tree diagrams should show 27 possibilities.

**TUESDAY**
1. 5.1 percent decline in population growth
2. 5
3. 36.3
4. x = 50
5. a. pounds or kilograms;
   b. ounces or grams;
   c. yards, feet, or meters;
   d. gallons

**WEDNESDAY**
1. All answers are true.
2. $2^6 \times 6^2$
3. b.
4. Answers will vary.
5. a. 5° F
   b. July & August
   c. The fluctuations are minimal.

**THURSDAY**
1. a. similar;
   b. neither congruent or similar;
   c. congruent
2. $5\frac{3}{4}$
3. $x = -\frac{2}{15}$
4. 3 hours, 48 minutes
5. Diagrams will vary, but should show that much of the volcano is below sea level.

**FRIDAY**
1. 338,549 more
2. Statements will vary. One possible statement: More people live in Honolulu than the sum of the population in the next nine largest cities.
3. About 300,000 more. (299,922)
4. Statements will vary. One possible statement: More than twice as many people live in Kaneohe than in Kiheio.
5. Circle graph or bar graph

# Week 19 (pages 59–61)

**MONDAY**
1. 12,855 m
2. Yes, both mountains have elevations greater than 12,000 feet.
3. a. no;   b. yes;   c. no;   d. yes
4. 1 in 4 chance for success
5. about $44\frac{1}{2}$ miles

**TUESDAY**
1. about 147 meters tall; Sentences will vary.
2. c.
3. 3.67
4. p = 0.85
5. Students' choices will vary. Check to see that total is within $5.00 of $200.00.

**WEDNESDAY**
1. 50,460 m up and 50,460 m down = 100,920 meters
2. a. >;      b. <;      c. <
3. m = –20
4. isoceles triangle
5.

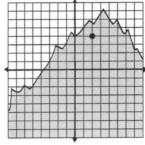

**THURSDAY**
1. No; The climb itself will take a little more than 80 hours, but the climbers will need to have breaks, eat, and rest during the 24-hour period.
2. $2.50 per meter
3. 24 possible permutations
4. 500 km.
5. 3

**FRIDAY**
1. 7,300 feet – 29.005 feet;
2. mean = 5,713 m, median = 5,790 m
3. Kilimanjaro, Everest, McKinley, Aconcagua
4. Everest, McKinley, Aconcagua
5. The elevation of Kilimanjaro is the median, so it is not greater than the median.

# Week 20 (pages 62–64)

**MONDAY**
1. 24
2. 1 in 4
3. z = 70
4. 700,000
5. 19 inches; two times around

**TUESDAY**
1. ounces
2. 1.5 ounces
3. 9.13, 9.2, 9.25, 9.26, 9.28
4. .89
5. No, she needs 50 cents more.

**WEDNESDAY**
1. a. 3, b. 16, c. 1, d. 0
2. –87
3. $P = \frac{5}{16}$
4. false
5.

**THURSDAY**
1. g = 62
2. a. .6; 60%
   b. .75; 75%
   c. .5; 50%
3. t = 999
4. true
5. 87,60 – 13,152 hours

**FRIDAY**
1. 8 mice
2. $3\frac{3}{4}$"
3. feet = number of mice x four; 60 feet
4. whiskers = number of mice x 2 (number of whiskers on one side); 30 whiskers
5. more than 50; Explanations will vary—the mother mouse will have 20 female babies, the first two female babies from the 20 female babies will have seven litters each with two female babies in each litter (14 female babies); the first two female babies from the 14 babies will have five litters with two female babies in each litter (10 babies); the first two female babies from the ten babies will have three litters with two female babies in each litter (6 female babies). That's 51 and the offspring of the second, third, fourth, litters haven't been added. A farmer who finds a nest of baby mice in January

# ANSWER KEY

needs to relocate the mice if he doesn't want to lose lots of corn.

## Week 21 (pages 65–67)

### MONDAY
1. 54 days
2. $10^7$
3. 5,613 high-rises
4. 25,193,448
5. a. cone; b. cylinder; c. square pyramid

### TUESDAY
1. 53 minutes
2. 84.42728
3. Answers will vary, but the vendor will probably use mental math or a calculator. He doesn't want to give a customer too much money in return so he won't estimate and he probably doesn't have a pencil and paper handy.
4. >
5. $3.00

### WEDNESDAY
1. a. –15; b. –64; c. 544
2. one out of three
3. 37.68 cm
4. 27 cubic feet
5. a. 50%; b. $18.00

### THURSDAY
1. a. $\frac{15}{4}$; b. $\frac{17}{2}$; c. $\frac{23}{8}$; d. $\frac{23}{5}$
2. a. $1\frac{2}{15}$; b. $\frac{1}{20}$
3. Student explanations will vary. 2,000
4. 63 windows
5. sides are 7 cm, 8 cm, 5 cm

### FRIDAY
1. 262 m.
2. 381 m — 247
3. Two; Trump World Tower, GE Building
4. Trump World Tower, One Chase Manhattan
5. Sentences will vary depending on the building chosen.

## Week 22 (pages 68–70)

### MONDAY
1. about 24, 800 miles
2. a. ÷; b. –; c. x; d. +
3. 135 degrees

4. 12
5. 92,751,450 miles; Statements about the relative distance will vary, but should reference the fact that the moon is much closer to Earth than the sun.

### TUESDAY
1. 22,750 square feet
2. 9 problems
3. a mile
4. a. .35;   b. 3.50;   c. .035;   d. .0035
5.

### WEDNESDAY
1. Congruent means exactly the same shape and size.
2. 1,608,000 or $1.608 \times 10^6$
3. p = –4
4. –3.7° F
5. a. c, b; b. b; c. a

### THURSDAY
1. Answers will vary. The mean surface temperature is the average temperature. Because the mean temperature is fairly low, there must be more cold places, or places with very cold temperatures, to compensate for places that have very warm temperatures.
2. 150,000,000 km
3. $\frac{18}{45}$, $\frac{2}{5}$, $\frac{12}{30}$
4. d.
5.

## FRIDAY
1. Answers will vary, but should address that the atmosphere must be very thin to be spread out over such a large area.
2. Nitrogen
3. bar graph or circle graph
4. Student graphs will vary. Check them for accuracy.
5. Answers will vary.

## Week 23 (pages 71–73)

### MONDAY
1. eighty-four million, seven hundred six thousand, three
2. 4
3. 162; 486; 1,458; Rule: n x 3
4. equilateral triangle
5. Categories, line plots, and conclusions will vary.

### TUESDAY
1. $21.86
2. 158
3. x > –1
4. $2.64
5. Measure student drawings for accuracy.

### WEDNESDAY
1. The chances of choosing two different kinds are better than the chances of choosing the same kind.
2. h = 32
3. $9.00
4. False
5. 490 square inches

### THURSDAY
1. nine cookies
2. x = $1\frac{2}{3}$
3. a. $\frac{4}{5}$; b. $\frac{2}{5}$; c. $\frac{1}{6}$
4. The cake weighs 32 ounces.
5. Three-quarters of the pie tin is filled.

### FRIDAY
1. Big Billy's total is $10.30. He gets $9.70 in change.
2. Grandma Jill's total is $7.00. She gets $3.00 in change.
3. Cheerful Cherrie's total is $17.40. She gets 60 cents in change.

4. Hungry Harry's total is $8.00. He will have $4.00 left.
5. Lovely Lilly's total is $167.25.

## Week 24 (pages 74–76)

### MONDAY
1. $6 \times 10^7$; $7 \times 10^7$; $13 \times 10^7$
2. Yes, one
3. About 1,008 bites per day
4. a. yes; b. yes; c. no
5. Nine combinations

### TUESDAY
1. about $168.00
2. about 54%
3. 3 x (10 + 9) = (3 x 10) + (3 x 9) = 30 + 27 = 57
4. 28 inches taller
5. Three chances in twenty $\left(\frac{3}{20}\right)$

### WEDNESDAY
1. 2 (horse visits) = dog visits; 4 visits for Pat's dog
2. –8, –6, 7, 8
3. –9
4. 50 minutes
5.

| 1 | 3 |
|---|---|
| 2 | 6 |
| 3 | 9 |

### THURSDAY
1. a. $\frac{4}{15}$; b. $\frac{16}{27}$; c. $\frac{21}{32}$
2. pints
3. number of animals = 8% x 45 + 45; 49 animals
4. 1,857,143 animals
5. 60 square feet

### FRIDAY
1. To find out whether the company made a profit in a specific month, add the expenses to the income.
2. The company made a profit in January, February, March, and June.
3. The company had a profit of $7,769.00.
4. $7,748.00
5. $6,453.00

## Week 25 (pages 77–79)

### MONDAY
1. 5:20 p.m.
2. 16
3. 45°

4. 27 times, strategies will vary

5. one in nine or $\frac{1}{9}$

**TUESDAY**
1. a.
2. 45
3. $24.21
4. Commutative Property of Addition
5. 1" long

**WEDNESDAY**
1. 1,000 watches
2. 7
3. b.
4. a. 28; b. –91
5. Cross out all sentences except the last three. He fell into bed at 8:00 p.m.

**THURSDAY**
1. $2\frac{5}{12}$
2. .64 inches per hour
3. 12 hours, 47 minutes
4. a. $\frac{1}{4}$ of the way around the clock;
   b. 6 times around;
   c. 420 times around the clock face
5. Check to see that chart is completed correctly. Reasons will vary.

**FRIDAY**
1. C = πd or 2πr, so C = 3.14(2 x 12')
2. A = πr$^2$ or 379.94 sq. ft.
3. 28,776 sq. ft.
4. 1.960
5. The minute hand would travel twice as far every hour. If the minute hand were two feet long, it would travel 4 x 3.14, or 12.56 feet per hour. If the minute hand were four feet long, it would travel 8 x 3.14, or 25.12 ft.

## Week 26 (pages 80–82)

**MONDAY**
1. $25 \times \frac{10^4}{10^{10}}$
2. 158
3. 240,000 or 2.4 x 10$^5$
4. true
5. $\frac{1\ mg}{50\ mg} = \frac{160\ lb}{}$

**TUESDAY**
1. $155 per year
2. a = 7
3. a. .4;
   b. 7.41666 . . . ;
   c. 5.25
4. 32 pints
5. No, without knowing the average life span (which cannot be computed from the range) the statement is not accurate.

**WEDNESDAY**
1. Rule: –9; 54, 45, 36
2. a. >; b. >; c. <; d. >
3. 200 treasures
4. a. –17; b. okay as is; c. 205; d. –15
5. a. (–4, 0);   b. (–5, 3);
   c. (0, 5);   d. (4, 3)

**THURSDAY**
1. 1,000 ants
2. 664 square meters
3. a. $5\frac{1}{3}$; b. $8\frac{1}{6}$; c. $7\frac{4}{9}$; d. $4\frac{11}{23}$
4. $\frac{5}{6}$ or .83 or 83%
5. Explanations will vary. $\frac{17}{40}$

**FRIDAY**
1. a. $5.00; b. $10.00; c. $5.00
2. about 20 cents per ant
3. the castle
4. Yes, the cost will be $37.08.
5. Responses will vary.

## Week 27 (pages 83–85)

**MONDAY**
1. 30,000
2. 847,447 New Zealanders under the age of 14.
3. 30.34
4. Rule: Add one more than was added the previous time. 24, 31, 39
5. b, c

**TUESDAY**
1. a. 8,000 + 700 + 40 + 2;
   b. 80,000 + 1,000 + 500 + 70 + 3;
   c. 9,000,000 + 400,000 + 2,000 + 4
2. x = 17.5
3. The hour-long boat excursion is less expensive.

(about $1.92 per minute)
4. The decimal pint is in the wrong place. 8 is the correct answer.
5. a. $12.00 NZ;
   b. $1.50 NZ;
   c. $30.00 NZ

**WEDNESDAY**
1. –3,754 m
2. c.
3. The probability of two rainy days is $\frac{8}{27}$.
   $c(r_0) = (\frac{1}{3})^3 = \frac{1}{27}$
   $c(r_1) = (\frac{2}{9}) = \frac{6}{27}$
   $c(r_2) = \frac{12}{27}$
   $c(r_3) = (\frac{2}{3})^3 = \frac{8}{27}$
4. 8
5. difference = approx. 101°F

**THURSDAY**
1. average for blue whale 130,500 kg; average for humpback 34,500 kg; difference = 96,000 kg
2. a. 87.5%
   b. 25%
   c. 80%
3. $3\frac{1}{4}$
4. 77
5. To convert metric measurements, multiply by the appropriate power of ten.

**FRIDAY**
1. the number of people on the set each day—complete information is not included.
2. 540 feet tall
3. 576 people
4. $313,400,000.00 and $546,900,000; 36.43%
5. $985,401.45 per day

## Week 28 (pages 86–88)

**MONDAY**
1.
```
    278
  x  69
   2502
   1668
  19,182
```
2. pyramid with a rectangular base
3. 134
4. 12 containers
5. Between 15 and 16 orbits

per day; about 5,840 orbits per year. Check to see that tables are completed accurately.

**TUESDAY**
1. about 236 miles; additional responses will vary
2. n = 10.8
3. $6 \times 10^6 + 4 \times 10^5 + 7 \times 10^4 + 2 \times 10^3 + 1 \times 10^2 + 4$
4. 243
5. one possible solution:

**WEDNESDAY**
1. a = 12
2. the length and the width of each panel; No, there is not enough information.
3. 1 in 2 chance
4. 22
5. a. point q
   b. point m
   c. point s
   d. point t

**THURSDAY**
1. To solve the problem the speeds must be expressed in the same unit. Either change shuttle travel to feet, or bullet travel to miles. The shuttle is faster. A bullet travels only about $\frac{1}{2}$ mile per second.
2. yes, both numbers are equivalent to one half
3. $\frac{1}{22}$
4. x ≥ –1
5. 96 squares

**FRIDAY**
1. length and diameter; the solar array
2. mass; Zarya FGB
3. 25%
4. 1,738 days
5. Range: 129 days – 196 days; Mean: 174 days

# ANSWER KEY

## Week 29 (pages 89–91)

**MONDAY**
1. 1 out of 3
2. 37.5 square inches
3. 700
4. x = 700
5. 625 visited before noon and the afternoon crowd was twice the size of the morning crowd

**TUESDAY**
1. 228 hours
2. 7,634, 5,456
3. $28.50
4. b
5. Answers will vary.

**WEDNESDAY**
1. It is not reasonable. One million four hundred two thousand nine hundred six is almost $\frac{1}{2}$ of 3,000,000.
2. a.
3. J and G, or G and K, or K and I, or I and J
4. c, b, a
5. Divide 24' by 3; 8 feet

**THURSDAY**
1. $\frac{5}{9}$
2. No, it was only five minutes longer.
3. $12\frac{1}{12}$
4. about 3056% of its newborn weight
5. a. $\frac{5}{6}$;   c. $\frac{4}{5}$;
   b. $\frac{1}{5}$;   d. $\frac{2}{5}$

**FRIDAY**
1. No, the four parts listed weigh almost 1,000 pounds and do not include the elephant's body.
2. 33.3 hours
3. 28 mph faster
4. The falcon is 6 times faster than the elephant.
5. Graphs will vary but should represent the following midpoints:
   prairie dogs ....6
   wolf...............6
   tiger ..............3
   leopard..........4
   kangaroo........1
   hedgehog .......4
   rhinoceros ......1

## Week 30 (pages 92–94)

**MONDAY**
1. 328,767,120 rides per day
2. $5 \times 3 \times 2^3$
3. 126 square cm.
4. 168
5. Yes. 1, 5, 9, 12, 16, 19, 22 = 84

**TUESDAY**
1. Answers will vary depending on the date activity is completed.
2. The speed of Sam's elevators should be underlined. Additional information about the amount of time spent on the elevator or the time needed to move from one floor to another is needed.
3. five hundred three thousandths.
4. 26.175
5. a. 4 minutes, 31.4 seconds;
   b. 28.6 seconds / 5 minutes as x / 60 min

**WEDNESDAY**
1. –15
2. Ninth floor; He passed by or visited 12 floors. (Floors 4, 5, 6, 7, 8, 9, 10, 11, 12, 13, 14, 15)
3. 3 out of five
4. a. cube; b. square pyramid
5. 5, 0, –6

**THURSDAY**
1. a. $4\frac{1}{5}$; b. $91\frac{9}{50}$
2. 400 meters per minute faster
3. $x = \frac{3}{5}$
4. 13 cents
5.

**FRIDAY**
1. 36 square feet
2. 252 square feet
3. 26 feet
4. 154 square inches
5. Answers will vary. Two possible answers are Passengers B and D and Passengers C and D.

## Week 31 (pages 95–97)

**MONDAY**
1. Comparisons will vary. One possible comparison: Fancy cat registrations in 2000 were 35,178 fewer than in 1990.
2. 58.5%
3. e
4. 24,705
5. 4,599 > 2,131 + 2,094; Maine Coon > Siamese + Exotic

**TUESDAY**
1. $70 \times 10^6$
2. .0834, .834, 8.34, 83.4, 834, 8,340
3. 0.05005
4. $5 \times 1.9 = 5 \times (1 + .9)$
   $= (5 \times 1) + (5 \times .9)$
   $= 9.5$
5. The total of Hazel's purchases is $38.80, making the Happy Cat Starter Kit $1.22 cheaper. If the items are of the same quality, the kit is a slightly better value.

**WEDNESDAY**
1. Three possible numbers: –3, –4, –3.5. Only whole numbers are integers, so it is not possible that all the numbers are integers.
2. Eight kittens in all
3. 4788 cats in Golden
4. 8,074.7
5. 19.625 square feet

**THURSDAY**
1. 690,773 households own cats
2. a. $\frac{2}{3}$; b. $\frac{3}{5}$; c. $\frac{1}{4}$
3. $42\frac{7}{8}$
4. $4\frac{1}{4}$; 4; $3\frac{3}{4}$
5. a. 16";   b. 8";   c. 10"

**FRIDAY**
1.

| 1 | 4 | 2 | 12 | 1 |
|---|---|---|-----|---|
| 5 | 20 | 10 | 60 | 5 |
| 10 | 40 | 20 | 120 | 10 |
| 20 | 80 | 40 | 240 | 20 |
| 50 | 200 | 100 | 600 | 50 |

2. p = 4 (number of cats)

3. t = (number of cats)
4. a. 13,808 paws;
   b. 280 million paws
5. 84 tails

## Week 32 (pages 98–100)

**MONDAY**
1. One possible correct answer: zebra
2. false
3. 33,852,906
4. Steve is the winner.
5. Check to see if graphs are correctly drawn. Observations will vary but should reference how close the competition was.

**TUESDAY**
1. 35 minutes
2. 57.46
3. between 5 and 6
4. 2 and 3
5. $18.87

**WEDNESDAY**
1. 235
2. –6 > –5
3. 225 squares on the board; about 3% of the total squares
4. 15 square feet
5. 39 E tiles played;
   5 U tiles played;
   2 A tiles played

**THURSDAY**
1. $\frac{3}{8}$" = 1 foot
2. x = 160
3. $7\frac{7}{8}$
4. Belle's average think time is 25 seconds longer.
5.

| $\frac{13}{50}$ | $\frac{24}{25}$ | $\frac{21}{50}$ |
|---|---|---|
| .26 | .96 | .42 |
| 26% | 96% | 42% |

**FRIDAY**
1. 1 out of 4
2. 1 out of 11
3. 1 out of 5
4. 2 out of 9
5. Answers will vary.

## Week 33 (pages 101–103)

**MONDAY**
1. 300,000 stars
2. 84

3. a. 2,876,000;
   b. 90,000;
   c. 521,000
4. Conclusions will vary, but should note that the galaxy is very large.
5. Danny can make his purchase.

**TUESDAY**
1. 45.72 meters
2. Dividing both sides of the equation by 24
3. x (multiply)
4. h = 3.6
5. a. 31,536,000 seconds in a year
   b. 31,536,000 x 299,792,458 or 9,454,254,955,488,000 meters in a year.

**WEDNESDAY**
1. 16 ($2) + 16 ($4) + 4 ($3) = total admission charges
2. a. –312; b. –63; c. 162
3. 21°
4. about 7
5.

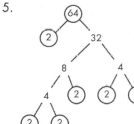

**THURSDAY**
1. $308.295 \times 10^{30}$
2. $\frac{38}{54}$
3. $2\frac{2}{3}$
4. a. $\frac{6}{25}$; b. $\frac{1}{5}$; c. $\frac{9}{14}$; d. $\frac{2}{3}$
5.

| 1 | 86 lbs. | 6,036 |
|---|---|---|
| $\frac{1}{6}$ | $14\frac{1}{3}$ lbs. | 1,006 |
| $\frac{5}{6}$ | $71\frac{2}{3}$ lbs. | 5,030 |

**FRIDAY**
1. about 120 light years
2. 53–360 light years
3. Mergrez
4. $\frac{53}{360}$
5. bar graph

## Week 34 (pages 104–106)

**MONDAY**
1. 12 x 104 or 120,000 quills
2. 70,000
3. pentagon
4. 7.36 square inches
5. A–A–B–B–A–A–B–B

**TUESDAY**
1. The cost is about $3.30 per week.
2. 4.725
3. 40.85
4. 9
5. Echidna—about .67 pounds per inch; Hedgehog—about .2 pounds per inch; Porcupine—1.1 pounds per inch

**WEDNESDAY**
1. a. – 25; b. 18; c. –10
2. <∡ acd and ∡ dcb
3. 11
4. 5:30 p.m.
5.

| | | | | X |
|---|---|---|---|---|
| X | X | | | X |
| X | X | X | | X |
| X | X | X | X | X |

| **1** | **2** | **3** | **4** |

| Porcupines Spotted | Frequency |
|---|---|
| 1 | III |
| 2 | III |
| 3 | I |
| 4 | IIII |

**THURSDAY**
1. The female will weigh about $3\frac{1}{3}$ lbs.
2. It represents a composite number, because any prime number plus one will be divisible by two.
3. It is stiff enough to break up logs and termite mounds when the echidna is searching for food. $\frac{1}{6}$
4. BIG, BGI, IBG, IGB, GBI, GIB
5. a. 36%  b. 76%  c. 52%

**FRIDAY**
   a. 11,860;  b. 3,354;
   c. 7,456;  d. 705;
   e. 234;  f. 247;

g. 34,416;  h. 29,309;
i. 7,800
They both float.

## Week 35 (pages 107–109)

**MONDAY**
1. 48 cm cubed
2. 416,150.2
3. a ≈ c
4. 1,000,000
5. One possible solution: Group 1: A, D, E; Group 2: B, C; Group 3: F

**TUESDAY**
1. 345 minutes
2. Number of shelves x 3 = number of supports
3. 2,426.52
4. 7.5 cm
5. Combinations will vary. One possible combination: paint roller, hammer, screw

**WEDNESDAY**
1. Its volume would increase eight times. A 2" cube has a volume of 8 inches cubed. A 4" cube has a volume of 64 inches cubed or eight times as much. A 3" cube has a volume of 27 inches cubed. A 6" cube has a volume of 216 inches cubed or eight times as much.
2. $\frac{1}{3}$ or one in three
3. 92
4. Check drawings to make sure students have drawn cylinders.
5. a. 21.43 Newtons; b. 16.7 Newtons

**THURSDAY**
1. $\frac{1}{4}, \frac{5}{16}, \frac{1}{3}, \frac{3}{8}, \frac{7}{16}, \frac{9}{16}, \frac{11}{16},$ $\frac{3}{4}, \frac{13}{16}, \frac{7}{8}, \frac{15}{16}, 1, 1\frac{1}{16}, 1\frac{1}{8}$
2. $\frac{3}{8}$
3. $\frac{6}{16}$ or $\frac{3}{8}$
4. $\frac{5}{8}$
5. $\frac{7}{8}$" bigger

**FRIDAY**
1. 100,000 joules
2. 690,000 joules
3. 750,000 joules

4. 40,000 joules
5. 62.5 joules

## Week 36 (pages 110–112)

**MONDAY**
1. 65%
2. c = 5
3. k = 13
4. $11\% = \frac{11}{100}$
5. 24 sq. units

**TUESDAY**
1. 2 p.m.
2. Eighty-six thousandths
3. The correct answer is 192.943.
4. The rule is +12. 55, 67, 79
5. a. $0.08 per month;
   b. $1.00 per month;
   c. about $36.67 per year

**WEDNESDAY**
1. x < 2
2. More than one is possible.

3. 41 feet
4. –9; 11; –17
5. 4 congruent triangles 5 similar triangles

**THURSDAY**
1. 24,762 inches or 2,063.5 feet
2. 60%
3. 40 kites
4. Since 49 equals seven squared and 21 equals seven times three, seven is a common factor of 49 and 21.
5. Patterns will vary. Check to see that one is A–B–B–A–B–B and one is A–B–C–A–A–B–C–A

**FRIDAY**
New Materials List
- 17" x 22" paper
- 16" piece of $\frac{1}{4}$" matchstick bamboo
- three $2\frac{1}{2}$" x 12' strips of plastic bags
- tape
- hole punch
- kite string